Richmal Crompton's William is known to those who have never even read the books featuring his anarchic exploits. His name has become a synonym for scruffy, adventurous and exuberant boyhood, but little is generally known of his creator, who always shunned the limelight. She remained so unobtrusive that many people, because of her unusual Christian name, still think that William's originator was a man. *Richmal Crompton: The Woman Behind William* provides a biographical picture of this witty and talented writer, and a celebration of her works. It will be appreciated by several generations of 'Just-William' fans throughout the world.

The book is illustrated with pictures of Richmal and her family, including the brother, nephew and grand-nephew who helped to inspire William's activities. It also includes pictures by Thomas Henry, the artist whose visual projection of William perfectly echoed and enhanced the mood of Richmal Crompton's stories.

Mary Cadogan wrote with Patricia Craig the critically-acclaimed *You're A Brick, Angela!* She has since become well-known as a writer and broadcaster on children's books and various aspects of popular culture. She has been an enthusiast of the William books for many years and has written several features on Richmal Crompton's work. She also wrote the entry about Richmal Crompton in the *Dictionary of National Biography*.

RICHMAL
CROMPTON

THE WOMAN BEHIND WILLIAM

"I've written some jolly good tales," said William, "An' I wouldn't mind helpin' you a bit."

RICHMAL CROMPTON

THE WOMAN BEHIND WILLIAM

Mary Cadogan

UNWIN PAPERBACKS

London   Sydney

First published in Great Britain by Allen & Unwin 1986
First published in paperback by Unwin® Paperbacks, an imprint of Unwin
Hyman Limited in 1987

UNWIN HYMAN LIMITED
Denmark House, 37-39 Queen Elizabeth Street, London SE1 2QB
and
40 Museum Street, London WC1A 1LU

Allen & Unwin Australia Pty Ltd
8 Napier Street, North Sydney, NSW 2060, Australia

Unwin Paperbacks with the Port Nicholson Press
60 Cambridge Terrace, Wellington, New Zealand

ISBN 0-04-440028-4

Printed in Great Britain by Cox & Wyman Ltd, Reading

CONTENTS

LIST OF PLATES

(between pages 78 and 79)

For Richmal and Paul Ashbee
with gratitude and affection

RICHMAL CROMPTON

ACKNOWLEDGEMENTS

Acknowledgements are due to Macmillan's Children's Books for permission to quote from the William stories, and to Hamlyn's for permission to use illustrations by Thomas Henry.

I also thank Richmal Ashbee for permission to quote from Richmal Crompton's other works, and Marjorie Fisher for allowing the use of Thomas Henry's colour portrait of William on the dust-jacket.

I wish to thank Mrs Joan Braunholtz, Miss Miriam Place, Lady Sybil Osmond, Mr David Schutte and Mr Jack Adrian for providing information about Richmal Crompton, or for lending me some of her more elusive books. My thanks are also due to Miss J. Plowman, the Headmistress of Bromley High School, and to Mr A. P. C. Pollard, the Headmaster of St Elphin's, for help with background research material.

I am very grateful to Miss Kate Ashbee for sharing her memories of her great aunt with me, and most of all I am indebted to Richmal and Paul Ashbee for their time, memories, patience and encouragement.

The following books were consulted:

WILLIAM – A BIBLIOGRAPHY
compiled by W. O. G. Lofts and Derek Adley
Published privately, 22 Scott Crescent, Harrow, Middlesex (1980)

THE STORY OF ST ELPHIN'S SCHOOL 1844–1944
by Margaret L. Flood
Published privately (1944)

ROYAL HOLLOWAY COLLEGE 1908–1914
by W. E. Delp
Published privately (1969)

SIXTY ODD YEARS
by Thos Rhodes Disher
Clerke and Cockeran Ltd. (1954)

SCHOOLGIRL VOICES 1883–1983
edited by Marie Bridge
Published privately by Bromley High School (1983)

TESTIMONY OF LIGHT
by Helen Greaves
World Fellowship Press (1969)

MARY CADOGAN
Beckenham, Kent
1986

INTRODUCTION

THE WOMAN BEHIND WILLIAM

"Just what I wanted," said the artist: "a dirty rapscallian of a boy with a crooked tie and a grimy collar."

It has often if not always accurately been said that behind every great man there is a great woman. Certainly that juvenile desperado *par excellence*, William Brown, owes his vivid fictional existence to a female writer. Richmal Crompton dreamed him up almost seventy years ago and by the 1940s his name had become part of the language, a synonym for scruffy and riotous boyhood. Since then, through further books, commercial spin-offs, and stage, screen, radio and television presentations, William's fame – or notoriety – has been consolidated.

Richmal Crompton, however, has remained unobtrusive. Even when she died in 1969 many William fans knew so little about her that, because of her unusual Christian name, they took it for granted that William's creator must have been a man.

It is time for this exceptionally talented author to be brought out from that shadowy place behind her anarchic but engaging brainchild and placed firmly in the limelight. She once wrote that 'the full life-story of anyone is, of course, more thrilling than a dozen novels'. This is particularly true of people whose lives are liberally spattered with action, colourful relationships or participation in public affairs. In Richmal Crompton's case the biographic excitements often lie well beneath the surface of events, and unfold only as diverse aspects of her inner life are uncovered. It therefore seems appropriate to present a portrait in depth of Richmal and a celebration of her works, rather than a detailed biography.

The stories which make up the first William books were written over six decades ago, but they retain their sparkle and satirical edge today. Their resilience is particularly surprising in view of the fact that Richmal considered her William tales as pot-boilers. Her ambition was to produce serious fiction for adults; she wrote some forty novels and several collections of short stories which, though extremely readable, never achieved the distinction of the William books. Some of these adult novels, however, provide insights into Richmal's real-life aspirations and achievements, especially when studied in juxtaposition with the exploits of her eleven-year-old anti-hero – the 'pot boiler' who was to become an archetype of the unbookish, adventurous outdoor boy.

Several generations of children have grown up in the long summer world of William, feeling that his village (which Richmal never named or precisely located) was real enough to be just around the corner. I spent my childhood at Bromley, in Kent, and always felt sure that William's world was just a short cycle ride away. I learned later that, in fact, Richmal Crompton's home was as near as that, but I never met her until I was grown up and working in London for the Infantile Paralysis Fellowship, a charitable organization which she supported. Disabled herself through polio, she came to the office several times. I felt too shy to talk to her about her William stories, but was impressed by her unpretentiousness, the humour that she so quickly extracted from bureaucratic absurdities, and the way she put everyone at ease in her company. She was immensely likeable – so likeable, indeed, that she is something of a biographer's nightmare. Despite attempts to provide a rounded-out and complete picture, it has been impossible to find anyone who has negative words to say about her!

CHAPTER 1

DEVOTED DAUGHTER AND STURDY SISTER

"If you'll give me two shillings," said William, "you'll never see me again after I'm twenty-one."

Richmal Crompton Lamburn was born on 15 November 1890, in a solid, roomy but unlovely house on the Manchester Road on the outskirts of Bury in Lancashire. 'Ray', as she became known to her family and friends, was the second child of the Revd Edward John Sewell Lamburn and his wife Clara (née Crompton). The Lamburns were already the fond and proud parents of another daughter, Mary Gwendolen (Gwen) who, just seventeen months older than Richmal, was always to remain close to her sister. The family soon expanded further; a son, Jack, was born to the Lamburns in April 1893. He inherited, somewhat infelicitously perhaps, the three names of his maternal grandfather, John Battersby Crompton, who in the previous year had surprisingly and without any apparent motive killed himself by taking prussic acid. This seemed an inauspicious way to name the young brother whose robust

1

childhood exploits were to provide the first inspiration for Richmal's lighthearted and exuberant William books.

Occurring when she was only eighteen months old, the untimely death of her grandfather had no impact on Richmal's life. Another family tragedy, however, left its mark on her affectionate and protective nature. The fourth Lamburn child, Phyllis Crompton, who was born in September 1894, died of whooping cough at the age of fourteen months. As well as feeling natural sisterly affection for Phyllis, Richmal always had a special penchant for babies, and this early bereavement almost certainly strengthened the bonds that already linked her to Gwen, her small brother Jack, and her parents.

Edward, Richmal's father, was a clerk in holy orders and licensed curate who had chosen to become a schoolmaster instead of taking a parish. With a degree in Latin, Maths and French, he taught at Bury Grammar School, and took temporary curacies during the holidays, partly to provide a country location for his family, partly to augment the Lamburn income, and, one suspects, also because – energetic, intellectual and with high ideals of service – he was something of a workaholic. At a certain level Edward seems to have been an embodiment of late Victorian ideas of cleanliness, godliness and stern paternalistic responsibility. He would break the ice on the local canal on winter mornings rather than abandon his daily dip. On a stipendiary curacy, to officiate at services, he walked ten miles and back every Sunday for several years. After teaching all day at Bury School he gave his children regular lessons at home, often using a big map of Europe that he'd conveniently installed in the bathroom. However, on top of all this, he was an extremely affectionate father, able, as well as preaching effective sermons, to regale his offspring with anecdotes that brought to life the people and cultures of classical times. Richmal, who was eventually to become a classics teacher, was particularly responsive to his stories of Greece and Rome, and rather engagingly, after going away to boarding-school with Gwen, she sometimes corresponded with her father in Latin.

There is no doubt that Edward succeeded in infusing his two inquiring and intelligent daughters with his own passion for learning. With Jack, however, it was a very different story. Less sensitive than his sisters to parental approbation or disapproval, Jack wasn't particularly interested in school work or private study, and took few pains to conceal this from his father. His response to homework was not dissimilar to that of William – whose school reports were the constant despair of his parents – when a dreadful godfather tried to persuade him to 'rub up' his maths in holiday time:

> William eyed him coldly. 'I don't think I'd better get muddlin' up on my school work,' he said. 'I shouldn't like to be more on than the other boys next term. It wouldn't be fair to them.'

Clara Lamburn, like her husband, had enormous vitality and strength of character. It was a family adage that she (like Gwen later on) would have made an ideal vicar's wife. Dedicated to the Christian virtues, she possessed a keenly developed sense of community responsibility, backed up by organizational ability. Like David's mother in *The Wildings*, and matriarchs in several of Richmal's other family sagas for adults, Clara was 'splendid – simply splendid' in the eyes of her family. It seems ironic that she should marry a man in holy orders yet be denied a parish and vicarage to reign over. This would not only have afforded Clara immense satisfaction but would have provided Richmal, a budding author from childhood, with superb character and social material for her future books. It is interesting that both in her William stories and in her adult novels she frequently parodies vicars with deadly accuracy and makes lots of short, sharp stabs at the distaff side of the established church:

> There was nothing in the world that the Vicar's wife enjoyed as much as speaking at Mothers' Meeting Conferences . . . or, indeed, anywhere at all . . .

Although Richmal was to relish the sending-up of child-detesting clerics and vicars' wives wearing insincere 'Sale of Work smiles', the Anglican faith that she accepted in childhood was important to her then, and subsequently.

This capacity to satirize causes and institutions that were precious to her was to become a feature of her writing, especially in the William stories. Frequently one feels that she is parodying herself as readily and as incisively as other people, and using William as a comic but nevertheless potent devil's advocate. Richmal's views are often expressed through her serious characters, while William is the mouthpiece of attitudes that are in direct opposition. In tastes, interests and ambitions he is almost always the direct antithesis of his creator. All this pinpoints the difficulties of trying to build up a picture of Richmal's opinions and aspirations from her writings. Nevertheless, when William's music-hall rumbustiousness is weighed against the drawing-room drama ingredients of her adult books, the balance, plus the repetition of certain themes, *does* provide clues to her multifaceted personality.

There is no doubt that in her early novels, such as *The Innermost Room* (1923) and *Anne Morrison* (1925) (which was dedicated to 'My Mother and Father'), she drew liberally on her own experience and relationships, but embellished these with touches of the imaginative flair that she later developed. In *Anne Morrison*, for example, the eponymous heroine physically resembles the young Richmal, who was slim, fair and fragile-looking. And Anne has a clerical/schoolteacher father who resembles Edward Lamburn in being an early-morning ice-breaking bather, in having a heavy sense of responsibility for the 'souls' (children) 'entrusted by God to his care', and in telling stories that filled Anne's 'baby world with a wonderful assemblage – with Odysseus, Perseus, Psyche and countless others'. He further resembles Richmal's father by keeping his children hard at it with out-of-school studies (Edward's bathroom wall map is pressed into action as one of the novel's props) and, again like Edward, finding his son's lack of academic ambition intensely frustrating.

Many more parallels can be pointed between the relationships of the fictional Morrisons and the real-life Lamburns, but it would be misleading to equate Richmal's early childhood too closely with Anne's. For example, Anne, like Richmal, has an overwhelming desire to live up to her father's lofty ideals but she is awed and frightened by him in a way that Richmal never was by Edward – whom in a juvenile letter she once cosily categorized as a 'darling' and 'my own sweet angle'(*sic*). Richmal had a vigorous sense of humour; Anne had none, and was inclined to morbid fancies about being unloved; 'the thick blackness' that enveloped her on such occasions was a measure of a psychological spinelessness that certainly didn't characterize Richmal then or at any time of her life.

From the upper front room of the Manchester Road house Richmal, Gwen and Jack could look out over a patchy panorama of houses, fields and factory chimneys. In 1896 their outlook changed for the better when the Lamburns moved into 4 Malvern Villas, a large terraced house in Chesham Road, Bury, which faced on to fields bounded by woods. The move brought them nearer to Clara's mother, Richmal Crompton, the widow of the grandfather who had committed suicide. She was the first of the family to bear this combination of names, although her unusual Christian name had been handed down over many generations. Mother of fourteen children (six of whom died in infancy), and grandmother to eight more, the matriarchal Richmal Crompton meant little to her juvenile namesake. Both Richmal and Gwen remembered family gatherings when 'Grannie' didn't even know which of her numerous grand-children she might be talking to. Fairly soon after moving into their new home the Lamburn children heard of the death of their paternal grandfather (whom they had never met) from a stroke, in 1898.

Life for Edward, Clara and their children at Malvern Villas assumed an even tenor. Clara, like her husband, was not afraid of hard work, and ran the large terraced house with the help of only one daily maid-of-all-work. This, of course, was at a time when it was common for middle-class and professional people to enjoy the benefit of full-time living-in domestic help. But money was not over plentiful Edward was supporting his mother, as well as his wife and children, and basically the family was dependent on his teaching salary, his temporary curacies, and some private coaching which added little to his income. This was slightly augmented by the addition to the household of two 'daily boarders' – boys attending Bury Grammar School who came to lunch (midday dinner) at the Lamburn home every day during term time. As well as imbibing refreshments, they were expected to absorb facts and figures. Never wasting the precious moment, Edward would often give them and his own children a dinner-time lesson. On several occasions they would sit in a row on the edge of the bath and from this uncomfortable perch receive geographical enlightenment from Edward and that bathroom wall map.

When they were small the Lamburn children all went to private or 'Dame' schools nearby, but they had plenty of time to play in the countrified areas around their home. (The houses in the terrace of Malvern Villas, like many Victorian town houses, had very little garden.) *Anne Morrison* provides a vignette of Anne and her younger sister Cathy similarly exploring local meadows and woodlands:

> Cathy found walks with Anne exciting but somewhat disturbing. Cathy was not imaginative. When she walked across a field she preferred on the whole just to walk across a field; but Anne was never content with things as they were. She had to spin a web of romance or terror over them.

Here we see a fictional evocation of Richmal the juvenile story-teller. Anne's approach to the natural scene is imaginative, high-flown and sometimes sentimental. She tells her sister about favourite places in language that seems to have come straight out of Bunyan's *Pilgrim's Progress*; little Cathy is introduced to 'the Field of Pleasure', 'the Road Dangerous', 'the Hill of Ogres', 'the Place of Peace', etc.

Writing for a different book at about the same time as when she produced *Anne Morrison*, Richmal Crompton shows us the delights of country life in a far more lively way: she is once again seeing things through the eyes of children – this time, through those of William and the Outlaws. In *William the Conqueror* (1926) they utilize their environment of fields and farms and woods to the full by 'ratting in Coben's barn', rabbit hunting in the woods with Jumble (William's beloved but not always particularly bright mongrel), crawling through ditches on their stomachs in the role of Red Indians engaged in tracking, damming a stream with mud, and sliding down one of Farmer Jenks's hay-ricks. In Richmal's words, 'they had raced and rambled and scrambled and wrestled and climbed trees and trespassed to their hearts' content'. They had also indulged in 'a heavy diet of unripe wild crab apples, unripe hazel nuts, green blackberries and grass (which they chewed meditatively between their more violent pursuits)'.

Exploits like these, which are so typical of William, Ginger, Henry and Douglas, could to an extent be indulged in by Richmal's brother Jack. But for her they were taboo, although she longed to participate in them. There is an element of wish-fulfilment in her creation of William's uninhibited capacity for physical enjoyment. Boisterous behaviour for girls was generally considered 'fast' in late-Victorian society and, apart from the usual social restrictions, Richmal was treated during the first decade of her childhood as an invalid. Slighter and quieter than the self-confident and outgoing Gwen, Richmal had to lie for periods on a backboard, as her parents nurtured the then common fear that their rather delicate-looking child might develop a curvature of the spine. She makes one of her spirited girl characters in *Felicity Stands By* (1928) comment that 'People who belong to the Victorian Age love chronic invalids. It was everyone's ambition in those days to be a chronic invalid.'

It certainly wasn't Richmal's – then, or at any time in her life. As she couldn't be running around the fields with Jack, she made the best of those times of enforced rest by reading, and dreaming up stories of her own. In an article about her childhood produced many years later she writes:

> Before I went to boarding school I used to edit a magazine called 'The Rainbow' (chiefly because I found a rainbow easy to draw on the cover with coloured chalks) . . . Its circulation was confined to two. I used to read it to my small brother and my beloved rag doll (she was called Lena) sitting on two doll-sized chairs in the attic. (*Preston Library Magazine*, 1964)

The attic at 4 Malvern Villas was one of Richmal's secret places. Like Louisa Alcott's Jo in *Little Women* (a book which the young Richmal encountered and admired), she sought refuge in the attic for her 'scribbling'. Her output included stories, poems and a diary. (One wishes fervently that the diarist urge had continued into adulthood. Sadly, apart from holiday journals, she left no diaries which might have been helpful to biographers and intriguing for her fans.)* Richmal's attic could be compared to William's 'old barn' as a headquarters and a place of sanctuary. The theme of secret worlds which constantly crops up in her adults' and children's books is most incisively explored in her first novel, *The Innermost Room* (see page 32).

There was liberalism as well as learning and affection in the Lamburn family ambience. During the Boer War, for example, Edward – who was never afraid of standing up for his principles against the pressure of public opinion – held and expressed pro-Boer views. His liberalism was further reflected in his determination, or rather his taking it for granted, that equally with his son his two daughters should receive the benefit of an excellent education. Jack became a pupil at Bury Grammar School – an arrangement which, with his father installed there as a teacher, was hardly ideal for the boy. However, it was financially advantageous, because for the sons of masters fees were not charged. At the age of eleven, Gwen went to board at St Elphin's Clergy Daughters' School at Warrington, where as the daughter of a curate she could be educated at reduced fees. Knowing that she would soon follow in her sister's footsteps, Richmal made the most of the time left to her at home, enjoying as fully as possible her dolls, her writing, her books – and her relationship with Jack.

Both Gwen and Richmal felt a strong sense of protectiveness towards their brother, possibly because he was younger and perhaps also because of the three Lamburn children he had the least scholastic ability, and most easily incurred Edward's displeasure. Richmal was Jack's protector in the imaginative sense, feeling empathy with him and worrying about his problems. Gwen's help was of a more practical nature: on at least one occasion she beat up a gang of boys who were bullying him. When Gwen went to boarding-school, Richmal felt especially close to Jack, even though he was now, of course, no longer literally her 'baby' brother. She had always liked younger children and babies – despite William's firmly and frequently

---

* Richmal Ashbee, née Disher (Richmal Crompton's niece) comments: 'At school she kept a sort of *public* diary in which all the girls and staff were disguised by animal nicknames, rather superficially. I believe she only destroyed this a few years before she died.'

expressed indifference towards them. In *William the Pirate*, he and the Outlaws are forced to take out Henry's baby sister. They accidentally lose her and her pram, and the story revolves riotously on their trying to find her, and, eventually, having to return three substitute babies whom they have managed to acquire to their rightful and indignant parents. Generally speaking William has only to spend five minutes with a baby for it to become covered in soot or dirt or chocolate; given longer in his company it is likely to be used as an object in one of the Outlaws' games, to be temporarily abducted or, at the least, mislaid.

As a child, Richmal liked to take babies out in their prams. Her true feelings for them are expressed in many of her adult novels. In *The Gypsy's Baby* (1954) she has no less than six women contend for the right to adopt a baby that is (quite obviously) soon to be born to the voluptuous but unmarried maidservant of the vicar's wife. In each case the would-be adoptive parent has first been deeply moved by the sight of the beautiful baby of a 'fair Romany' who has encamped near the village:

> Golden and dimpled, with gleaming curls, it was the baby of Baltraffio's Madonna, except that its eyes were . . . azure blue . . . Naked but for a short woollen vest, it waved chubby arms and legs, laughing and crowing at the swarthy little girl who knelt by it, tickling its cheeks with a swinging tassel of catkins.

The madonna image is repeated when, through the tenuous influence of the gypsy's baby, a diversity of love-starved characters find the key to the unlocking of their emotions and to embarking on meaningful relationships.

Richmal grew increasingly alarmed at the gulf that was developing between Jack and his father. Being at the same school as 'Lammy' (the nickname which Edward's pupils bestowed upon him) meant that Jack could rarely escape his father's eagle and elevating eye. Paul, who is brother to the fictional Anne Morrison, finds himself in exactly the same predicament. He too has to attend the school where his father teaches; like Jack he is unacademic but constantly chivvied by his father to do better at his studies. As Paul confides to Anne, being a pupil at his father's school is 'jolly awkward', to say the least. (Paul is forced by his father to read the leading article of *The Times* every day, in order to improve his written style and spelling; it is more than likely that Edward applied the same literary discipline to Jack.)

Amongst a collection of postcards that Richmal kept throughout her life is one from Jack (when he was ten, and away recuperating at a Yorkshire hydropathic establishment) to Edward. It says much about their relationship. Jack writes about his enjoyment of walking and climbing hills, and asks to be allowed to stay on for a few days: '. . . it would be for the better, it is so invigorating here. I think I should work all the better for it. *Please let me*. There are tons of places I want to walk to here.' These few lines, written long ago in childish handwriting, vividly convey the quintessential conflict between the outdoor boy and a bookish, academic parent. But, happily, however 'cribbed, cabined and confined' Jack sometimes felt, he managed to find time and opportunity for the lively enterprises that caught Richmal's imagination sufficiently to inspire her, years later, to create William.

She took the business of being Jack's sister pretty seriously. Insights into the importance to her of this relationship can be gleaned from her many descriptions of the sisterly role in a variety of her adult novels. In *The Wildings* (which is appropriately dedicated 'To My Brother'), eighteen-year-old Clare and her older brother David tend to harp on their affection for each other in a manner that is obtrusive, if not unnatural. Clare compares every man she meets unfavourably with David. She is impressed by a handsome stranger until

by him she set David, her standard of perfection, and he seemed to fade at once into nothingness. In spite of his beautiful clothes and wonderful manners, he couldn't stand for a minute beside David. And she was glad – glad that he was so nice and yet that David still reigned supreme. Subconsciously she feared meeting someone who, when put with David, would make David fade away . . .

There is a great deal more in this vein, and David feels a similar intensity about Clare. Her 'shy, rather frightened smile brings a catch to David's heart', and even after he is married (to Hero, a much more satisfying and balanced character than Clare) his sister's hold on him remains limpet-like: 'There was no-one in the world quite like Clare.' On one occasion, when Clare is visiting them, Hero – not surprisingly piqued at playing gooseberry to her own husband and his sister – comments:

'No-one could ever be to you what Clare is, could they?'

He hesitated. He knew what she wanted him to say, and for a minute he was tempted to buy peace by saying it. Then he said firmly, 'No'.

'Why not?' she said with the stormy calmness that he knew so well. 'What does Clare give you that – other people can't?'

'I've told you,' he said impatiently – 'it's a bond that's different from any other bond – the bond of brother and sister...'

'I've known brothers and sisters who haven't a good word to say for each other.'

'... They've missed something, that's all I can say.'

Of course, one brother-and-sister combination who in David's words 'miss something' and in Hero's 'haven't a good word to say for each other' is that of William and Ethel Brown. Here once again we find Richmal Crompton in the William saga exactly reversing sentiments that recur in her stories for adults. Ethel is a fatuous and work-shy 'flapper', whose red-gold hair and long-practised eyelash flutterings ensnare (in the course of the thirty-nine William books) every unmarried male resident of the village and every eligible bachelor who visits it. The only fly in her seductively perfumed ointment is William, who, even when he is not consciously waging guerilla warfare against her, manages constantly to upset, embarrass and infuriate her. ('But William,' said Mrs Brown, 'how did you think it was going to help anyone to say Ethel had epilepsy and consumption?') Ethel is driven to the lengths of suggesting to her mother that William ought to be sent away to an orphanage, and when the ever-placid Mrs Brown explains that this is impossible because he isn't an orphan Ethel wails 'But he's so awful! . . . He's so unspeakably dreadful!'

One of Ethel's most frequent comments about her younger brother, especially at meal times, is simply 'His manners!' – in tones of utmost contempt. There is always, too, some malicious relish in her voice when she tells William of the retribution that is likely to follow his latest wrongdoings – or even when she is merely calling out through the dusk 'William! Mother says it's long past your bedtime and *will* you come in . . .'

There is a counterbalancing antagonism in William's attitude towards his sister, whom he often categorizes as 'interfering and bad-tempered and stingy, and everything that an ideal sister should not be'. He is always completely at a loss to understand what his sister's legion of male admirers see in her:

> Suddenly someone appeared in the doorway. To the young man it was as if a radiant goddess had stepped down from Olympus. The barn was full of heavenly light. He went purple to the roots of his ears.
>
> To William it was as if a sister whom he considered to be elderly and disagreeable and entirely devoid of all personal charm had appeared. He groaned . . .

All this, of course, redresses the balance of Richmal's eulogies on the brother-and-sister theme in her adult books, but there was never any ambivalence about her warm feelings for Jack, which lasted from childhood to old age.

The close-knittedness of the Lamburns is reflected again and again in Richmal's family sagas, which explore many aspects of love and jealousy between mothers and sons, fathers and sons, and between siblings. In *Anne Morrison*, Aineen is the fictional counterpart of Clara Lamburn – gracious, capable, matriarchal and 'magnificent' (another word used by Gwen and Richmal to describe their mother). Aineen's son Paul, who appears to have a great deal of Jack in him, adores his mother, but, as we have noted earlier, feels distanced from his father. He is jealous of the latter's place in Aineen's affections and asks her whom she loves best in the world. Aineen replies, 'Daddy' – and that next, of course, come the children. Paul presses his point:

'Does Daddy love you better than anything?'. . .

'Better than anything. Next to God. He'd do anything in the world for me . . . Anything that was right.'

'I love you more than Daddy does. I love you better than God. I'd do anything for you, even if it was wrong and bad.'

'Hush . . . Paul, darling.'

He laid his flushed face against her cool hand.

There is a marked diminution of this mother-and-son intensity in the Brown family. We are often told that Mrs Brown has a rather touching faith in William's latent powers of goodness, and that William, who despises most girls and women, makes a grudging exception of his mother. But moments of overt affection between them are rare. When William *does* appear to show fondness for his mother there is usually an ulterior motive, as when in *William the Pirate* he seeks her company in the garden in order to provide himself with an alibi:

Mrs. Brown was deeply touched. William had always seemed to her to be sadly lacking in that pretty affectionateness that makes some children so attractive. As a toddler he had invariably answered 'Villum' when she asked him whom he loved best in all the world. She would always remember in future that he had asked her to come out and sit near him while he worked in his little garden . . .

(Actually, he's *not* working; he's discovered a way of making doorbells peal constantly in the next-door house, to drive to demoniac distraction an unpleasant neighbour against whom William has several scores to pay off.)

The juxtaposition of these mother-and-son scenes from *Anne Morrison* and *William the Pirate* illustrates Richmal's long-continuing (but perhaps unconscious) technique of sending up her domestic dramas in the William books. The subject of estrangement, or simply gulfs in understanding, between father and son was a prominent one in both types of saga. The over-dutiful father (probably based on Edward) whose zealousness inhibits his son is often found in Richmal's adult novels. In the William stories the gulfs are equally wide, but expressed in happily facetious or ironic terms. Mr Brown rarely shows affection towards his younger son. His only regular round-the-home pursuits (in which he hates to be interrupted) are immersion in daily and evening newspapers and some desultory gardening (the serious work is, of course, done by a paid gardener). Unlike Edward Lamburn, he even caustically brushes off his son when, inspired by a sudden infatuation for his pretty teacher, Miss Drew, he starts doing homework and asks for help with it.

Especially in retributive encounters, Mr Brown casts constant 'pearls of sarcasm' upon William which float far above his head. Even when father and son *do* concur about something, there are unbridgeable divides in communication. For example, when William's infatuation with Miss Drew (and his interest in doing homework) fades, he explains to his father that he's given up doing extra work because Miss Drew doesn't know what she means; Mr Brown remarks sardonically that this is always the trouble with women, and tells his wife that William's idol has 'feet of clay'. William, literal-minded as ever, rejoins that he thinks her *feet* are all right; the trouble is, she simply can't 'talk straight . . . 'Sides, when they make folks false feet, they make 'em of wood, not clay.'

We are often told that William regarded the adults in his family as 'stumbling blocks placed in his path by a malicious fate', and the theme of generation gaps (first suggested to Richmal by differences in the aspirations of her father and brother) was to become the subject of some of her most perceptive and entertaining writing. In the very first William book, *Just William*, Mr Brown observes to an associate in whose home he is dining that 'the human boy is given to us as a discipline. I possess one. Though he is my own son I find it difficult to describe the atmosphere of peace and relief that pervades the house when he is out of it.' When Mr Brown's host comments that he'd like to meet this particular boy, William's father replies uncompromisingly: 'I prefer people who haven't met him. They can't judge me by him.' (He little guesses that at that very moment William, who has run away from home, is working below stairs in his host's house as a boot-boy. He is soon to disrupt the dinner party by charging wildly into the room streaked with boot-blacking and knife-powder, and pursued by an apoplectically furious butler.) This is domestic comedy at its most scintillating, inspired and strongly coloured by Richmal's childhood days in Bury.

CHAPTER 2

SCHOOLDAYS AND SECRET WORLDS

"I've explored places where no white man ever set his feet before,"
said William.

Richmal started her boarding-school days at St Elphin's, the
Clergy Daughters' School in Warrington, Lancashire, in 1901,
when she was in her eleventh year. At the time the excitement of
commencing a new century was still in the air; female
emancipation in the shape of the elusive vote was being
campaigned for with increasing urgency, and the idea of serious
education for girls was beginning to blossom and bear fruit.

Richmal too flowered at St Elphin's. The more sensitive
aspects of her nature found communal life a difficult challenge
in some respects, but it offered the compensations of lively
companionships, schoolgirlish 'larks', sport and theatricals – all
of which Richmal thoroughly enjoyed. She found satisfaction
also in the high academic standards expected of pupils at St
Elphin's, and had no difficulty in attaining these. Her
appreciation of the school is well conveyed in the following

poem which she wrote for the *St Elphin's Magazine* in 1907, when she was approaching the end of her schooldays.

S tand up for S. Elphin's, ye old girls and new,
A nd keep its name sacred whatever you do;
I t's a name whose traditions are sound and intact,
N ever sully or stain it by word or by act.
T hrough school life and after let this be your rule—
E 'er to cleave to your motto and honour your school,
L earn to fight with a will and you're certain to win,
P lay up for S. Elphin's through thick and through thin.
H er honour is sacred and true, every bit;
I n everything show her you've courage and grit,
N ever forgetting the time-honoured call—
S aint Elphin's for ever!—the best school of all!

There are touches in this of the spiffing schoolgirl spirit ('all grit and grind, and blade straight to the narrowest edge') that Angela Brazil began to immortalize around the time that Richmal's poem appeared in print. It is interesting to reflect that she was one of that generation of schoolgirls which inspired Angela, the founding mother of the genre, to create the girls' boarding-school story.

Richmal arrived at the Clergy Daughters' School looking rather less like the traditional image of Alice in Wonderland than she had done when she was little. She still had long, light hair, a slim build and a pale, slightly dreamy look. But happily the backboard had become a thing of the past, and at Warrington she was fit enough to plunge into the games and sport that were then popular (and sometimes even a positive mania) at girls' schools. In the appropriate seasons, St Elphin's offered hockey, tennis and cricket. Richmal's favourite of these was hockey, at which she became adept, although, as she wrote many years later, there was a distinct haziness at the school about the rules of the game. The pitch, too, was unorthodox:

... we had no games mistress ... and only the vaguest idea how to play it. The girls who wanted to play assembled on the playground, two girls picked up sides and out of these the correct players were assigned to the correct positions, while the rest played as 'fishes', darting about the field and hitting the ball as best they could in the right direction when they got the chance. The elder girls wore skirts that reached their ankles, and beneath them voluminous cambric petticoats tied round the waist by tapes. It was no unusual thing for one of these petticoats to escape its moorings and descend to the ground, and the game would be held up till the garment was more securely fastened. The game was held up, too, whenever a particularly vigorous 'swipe' sent the ball into a sluggish stream – fairly shallow but quite broad – which we called the 'moat' and which ran alongside the playground. Then all the players would gather on the bank to fish for the ball with their sticks, stirring up the mud and releasing a most unwholesome stench but seldom managing to retrieve the ball. (Preston Library Magazine, 1964)

This description, too, conjures up images straight out of the Angela Brazil sagas. It is especially reminiscent of a story in which a girl who is supposed to be a dab hand at cricket 'catches the balls in her skirts'! Incidentally, Richmal Crompton didn't rate Angela Brazil's stories of Edwardian school life very highly, for she went on record, years later, as saying that the boys' school had inspired some great chroniclers but that 'the girls' school classic remains to be written. We have nothing to set against *Tom Brown's Schooldays* or even *The Fifth Form at St Dominic's*' ('Writing for Children', *The Writer*, October 1952). She went on to say that the truly authentic girls' story would surely eventually spring from a day-school setting (see page 56). So Angela Brazil and her imitators and successors were, in Richmal's view, inadequate to their task. What a pity it is that she never tackled the girls' school story herself!

Gwen, of course, had already blazed the St Elphin's trail before Richmal went there. Her presence and her understanding of school regimes were immensely helpful to the younger sister.

The school building at Warrington was a vast, rambling former convent which, although lacking the amenities of a purpose-built educational establishment, at least offered scope for the imagination:

Unexpected steps led up or down into nearly every room, the walls were so thick that half a dozen girls could curl up comfortably on the window-seats and there were legends of secret passages that we tried in vain to discover. The place was supposed to be haunted by a nun and the more imaginative of the pupils swore that they had seen her at the end of some dim-lit corridor or flitting through a dormitory at night. (*Preston Library Magazine*, 1964)

The legend of the spectral Sister helped to stir a rich seam in Richmal's fantasy writing. Still 'scribbling' stories and poems as she had done at home, she later commented:

After I went to the school, ghosts began to figure in my stories, particularly as my sister and I shared a dormitory cubicle that had a mysterious door high in the wall far beyond our reach with no means of getting up to it. We longed to penetrate the mystery and on the last day of one term (feeling that we would soon be beyond the reach of punishment) decided to do so. I was set to keep cave at the dormitory door and my sister and her friends piled up the dormitory furniture (at great risk to life and limb) till they could reach the door. They managed at last to climb up to the door. They managed to push it open but it was a great disappointment. All it contained was a horse trough full of mouldy books and some dead birds!

Richmal's interest in the supernatural, which began in her schooldays, remained intense over the years. Her literary treatment of ghostly situations ranged from the comic and iconoclastic (in her William books) to a selection of short stories (*Mist*, 1928) which produced a genuine *frisson*.

'I can think,' [William] went on meditatively, 'of quite a lot of people I'd like to haunt when I'm dead – ole Markie [his Head Master] an' Farmer Jenks [another of his traditional enemies] an' people like that. It'd be more *fun* being a ghost than *anythin'* – even a pirate.'
    'I dunno,' said Douglas, 'they can't *eat*. . .'

19

Without exception, of course, ghostliness in the William stories emanates from skulduggery (William's) rather than the supernatural. One can be sure that when a horrified house-parlour-maid hurtles across her mistress's drawing-room burbling about 'vishuns' or 'hastral bodies' William is somehow at the bottom of her optical illusions. He is on one occasion mistaken for an evil spirit, and the subject of an improvised but effective exorcism. In trying to implement a resolution to rescue people who might be held under duress, the Outlaws incur the wrath of many respectable local residents as they peer furtively into windows, looking for bound victims being forced by torture to sign away their worldly goods. One elderly inhabitant 'suddenly seeing William's face with his nose flattened whitely against her window-pane' thinks that he is an evil spirit, and tries to exorcize him by the simple method of opening the door and flinging a Prayer Book through the darkness in his direction. 'Because it was a heavy Prayer Book and the lady's aim was sure, as an exorcism it was wholly successful . . .'

In *Mist*, Richmal's wide-ranging and compelling suspense stories for adults are atmospherically charged with murder, moonshine and murkiness. They are often rooted in domesticity, or in someone's oppressive fascination with an old house or garden, and are not only skirmishes with the supernatural but tangles of love and dependence and jealousy. The ghosts really *are* grisly: one manifests as a strange and sobbing presence, one as 'a half-seen flicker of light', and another as merely 'a breath' or an influence. This sense of something creepy under her normally clear-headed attitude to life crops up in several of Richmal's adult stories which are not specifically concerned with the supernatural. In *The Innermost Room*, Bridget, as a little girl, has to face a recurring, long-repressed horror which began when she and her sister Gloria encountered a man wheeling a hand-cart:

There had been something on the cart – something covered over with a cloth . . . At first they didn't take much notice of it. Then, just as they paused, they saw something hanging down the side of it from under the covering. It was a man's hand. They could see the hand – white and wet – and part of the shirt-sleeve dripping, dripping as it went along ... And over Bridget's soul had come a sudden horror – a sickening realisation of nightmare depths beneath the clear calm surface of life, beneath the violets and primroses and wonders and games and people who laughed and talked.

For Bridget, the horrific sight of a drowned man and her fearful response to it are summed up as 'the enemy', which she becomes agonizingly anxious to avoid or circumvent whenever there is a danger of a similarly disruptive happening or psychic shock occurring.

There are indications that Richmal, who was extremely sensitive and imaginative, might have shared some of the named and nameless fears that gripped her fictional characters. Her fascination with the macabre, however, was generally held in check by her keen eye and ear for the comical nuances which she could spot in both high-flown and humdrum situations, as this further extract from the article on her schooldays indicates:

The old garden played a great part in our lives. I and some of my friends had formed a secret society whose background was the garden and whose aims were mainly literary. Each week the members wrote a story or poem and posted them beneath the roots of an ancient tree in the garden. (I have no idea why we posted them there!) On the day of the meeting we took out the papers, gathered together in a secluded part of the garden, read our efforts aloud, voted for the best and agreed on the subject of next week's effort. The winner wore a badge – a bow of purple ribbon fixed onto a safety pin – for the week of her triumph. (I seem to remember that we had a secret password.) We imagined that the whole school was consumed by envious curiosity about our activities, but probably they never even noticed them.

Richmal seems to have transmogrified this schoolday secret-society experience into the secret poetry group which William's elder brother, Robert, formed with some of his contemporaries in *William in Trouble*. Every member had to compose a poem to be read aloud at each meeting, so that the best could be chosen, and its creator awarded 'an ornate badge'. Richmal pokes fun at the abysmal poetry produced by Robert and co. and at William's attempts (despite his running vendetta against his brother) to get Robert made Poet of the Week.

William also, of course, forms secret societies for specific purposes, and in the interests of general expediency. Indeed, the Outlaws themselves constitute such a society, of whose existence their parents know nothing. To Mr and Mrs Brown, for example, Ginger, Henry and Douglas are simply diverse boys with whom William sometimes plays, and not part of a corporate body of boyhood.

In the article on her schooldays Richmal writes:

The largest room was 'the big schoolroom' and in this four classes were always held simultaneously, one in each corner, so that if you were bored by your own lesson you could listen to one of the others. The dreaded Headmistress sat on a small platform behind a desk at one end. She appeared to be busy with some work of her own but had eyes and ears that missed nothing and she would every now and then pounce with sudden ferocity on some young offender, striking terror into the hearts of teachers and taught alike.

The 'dreaded Headmistress' was Miss Kennedy, one of St Elphin's several distinguished principals.

This schoolroom scene finds anarchic echoes in several William stories:

William and the Outlaws sat on the back row of the School Hall, carelessly cracking nuts and surreptitiously scattering the shells under the bench on which they sat . . . The Outlaws never listened to the Head Master when he was making a speech. His speeches were generally exhortations to lead a better life, and the Outlaws considered that this did not concern them because they'd often tried leading better lives and had found them more fruitful of complications than their normal lives of evil-doing.

William further enlivened the avenues of academe by introducing

22

mice into the classroom, flicking inky blotting-paper pellets at his enemies and playing ruler-and-rubber games of cricket with his friends. In class he tried always to sit in the back row, and, unlike Richmal, to while away the hours 'for which his father had paid the Education Authorities substantial sums'.

In 1904, after a severe outbreak of scarlet fever and the discovery of suspect drains, the old Warrington premises were condemned. Girls and staff moved to Darley Dale, near Matlock in Derbyshire, into a building which had once been a hydro-pathic hotel. In Richmal's words, 'It was larger and healthier and we loved the moors, but – we missed our ghost.' St Elphin's (which still thrives today) commanded views over undulating countryside and was an expansive place. The wood-panelled entrance-hall and winding staircase were a signal of the elegance and dignity of the whole building. Big and airy without being coldly cavernous, and far better equipped than the former Warrington convent, it provided a perfect setting for a girls' residential school. (It had proper hockey pitches, too.)

St Elphin's was academically progressive, with firm emphasis on careers, on classics, and universalism in education. Richmal developed a passion for classics. Dips into the school magazine during the period she spent there indicate her repeated successes – 'R. Lamburn. Pass. Distinguished in Latin', etc. – as well as the interest that she and Gwen took in drawing and dramatics:

Now we come to another original [play by] VA., the authoress in this case being Ray Lamburn. This had not much plot, but was mainly a skit on many school customs and incidents. Ray herself was a most undignified king, who could not possibly keep his accounts, even with the incompetent help of his chancellor (Dorothy Appleyard) There was a princess (Dorothy Birch Jones) who married a shepherd (Kathleen Thomas), and a witch in the person of Gladys Wilson. (*St Elphin's Magazine*, 1907)

The issue of the magazine which reported the production of Richmal's royal skit also mentioned that Gwen Lamburn made 'a stalwart' balcony-scene Romeo in a production by the lower

23

sixth. This, like Richmal's playlet, was presented on the occasion of the school's All Saints' Day holiday. In 1907 Richmal was a member of the school magazine's 'energetic' committee, as well as being a regular and enthusiastic contributor. She was the recorder (in debunking verse) of several school outings and functions, and the following poem, which seems to owe some inspiration in metre and mood to Lewis Carroll's 'The Walrus and the Carpenter', appeared in the magazine in 1909. (Like her other contributions it was signed 'R.C.L.'; she did not adopt the pen-name of Richmal Crompton until much later.)

OUR PICNIC

THE day was very bright and fine, the sun was in the sky
(I do not know the reason, so I cannot tell you why).
We were picnicing to Dove Dale for our usual mid-term fête,
And at ten a.m. in char-a-bancs we started off in state.
To see the sights of Dove Dale every one of us was pining;
For two whole hours we drove along, and still the sun was shining.
'But, oh, my friend, is that a cloud, so small and far away?
And can this be a drop of rain? O tell me, friend, I pray.
Oh, can this be a summer shower? What mean these dismal fogs?'
To tell the plain unvarnished truth, it's raining cats and dogs.
We all put up our 'brollies,' and we all put on our 'macks,'
And little streams of water soon are trickling down our backs.
Still, undepressed, we pass the time with endless jokes and tales;
But after, say, an hour or so, our conversation fails.
For a 'brolly' to the left of me has poked my hat awry,
And a 'brolly' to the right of me is digging out my eye
(And still the rain comes pouring down, and still the sky is black),
A 'brolly' just behind me is now dripping down my back.
But do you see, my friend, the clouds are lifting over there?
(The 'brolly' to my right is now entangled in my hair);
We hope that it will soon clear up, alas! we hope in vain,
For nothing happens all the day but rain and rain and rain.
We reach the Peveril of the Peak, and there we have our lunch.
(The shapes of all our hats would be a subject fit for 'Punch'!)
They give us a piano and a room in which to play,
And the noise we made that afternoon was heard a mile away.
Then after tea we think it time we started home again,
So we don our 'macks' and 'brollies' as defence against the rain;

We dash through every watery road and every muddy street,
Causing infinite amusement to the people whom we meet.
The 'brollies' all around me are quite blocking out my view,
But still, in spite of all, the rain succeeds in coming through.
Then, home once more, each drenched maid up to her dortoir goes,
We wring the water from our hair, and change our dripping clothes.
And you, my friends, perhaps will be surprised to hear me say,
That some of us, in spite of all, enjoyed this curious day;
Perhaps it was the dampness or the blackness of the sky,
I do not know the reason, so I cannot tell you why.

One of her stories for the magazine in 1906 features her favoured subject of ghosts – the spectres of girls and mistresses who, one hundred years on, revisit the school on the centenary of an occasion when each St Elphinite had planted 'her own particular tree ... on the stretch of waste-land outside the playing-field':

> ... another ghost [was] rapidly approaching. It was tearing its hair and uttering cries of horror and despair. In one hand it held a Latin Grammar and in the other a history of Rome. It drew near me, and, with surprise, I recognised the shade of Miss Flood.* In a broken harassed voice it addressed me. 'Oh! Why *will* they say 'monĕret' and 'shuus', when I've told them to say 'monēret' and 'suus'!'

The humour of 'The Planting of the Tree' meanders over a range of schoolgirlish jokes, from Greek and Latin to gregory-powder, and from algebra to aperients. Further gleanings from the St Elphin's magazines are that one of Richmal's companions in larks and learning was called Margaret Thatcher (but not, of course, the girl from Grantham), who in company with Gwen and several other students won an annual £5 prize in 1906. The same issue of the magazine records that Gwen gained a Class III pass in the Oxford Local Examination in July 1906, and showed 'sufficient merit to receive a certificate qualifying for admission to University Examination for degree of B.A. and B.Mus.' However, Gwen failed to win the university scholarship that was

* This formidable lady was to play a censorious part in Richmal's life later on: see page 49.

essential in those fee-paying days, and after leaving school took an external degree, followed by commercial qualifications. (Richmal, however, *did* manage to become a full-time university student; see page 35).

As we have seen, Richmal was erudite enough when still a schoolgirl to exchange postcards in Latin with her father. Her main fictional hero, however, not only lacked a bent for Latin but had a somewhat bizarre approach to English, as the following passage indicates:

> They staired at each other in garstly raige you cink of inickwitty said the dubble pail with gilt you blaggard steaped in krime said the king in a nobel voice but bewear your dume is ceiled and your days are gnumbered . . .

Richmal's feeling for the structure of the language was impeccable, but she never developed the perfect copperplate handwriting that distinguished Edward's postcards to her whilst she was away at school. She had learned to write at the small local private school she had attended in her pre-St-Elphin's days, and her jerky scrawl, which never improved, was suggestive of a mind that thought too quickly for the passage of pen across paper.

Sometimes Richmal couldn't resist the impulse to let William loose on a conventional girls' school, cast in the St Elphin's mould. Generally speaking, his entanglements with such establishments heaped chaos upon confusion, and ended infelicitously for himself. On one occasion he enters the confines of a girls' boarding-school by accident, to be roped in by the art mistress as a model for her painting class (she thinks he's the gardener's boy).

> A girl in the front row gave a shudder.
>
> 'Isn't he *dirty*?' she said.
>
> 'Never mind,' said the mistress, 'I want you to draw him as he is – just an ugly, dirty, little boy.' She had apparently looked upon William as something as inanimate as a plaster cast, but the ferocious glare which he now turned on her informed her that he was not . . .

He is restrained from indignant flight only by his sudden attraction to one of the girls who has 'dimples and dark curls'. She proves his undoing, however, when later on she asks him to substitute for her in the school play that afternoon so that, engulfed by homesickness, she can go and see her family. Unfortunately her role in the play is hardly appropriate for William: it is that of 'Fairy Daffodil'. But so strong are William's chivalrous intentions that he is prepared to undertake even this unpalatable part. The girl at first protests that he doesn't look like a fairy:

> 'I could make myself look like one,' said William grimly. 'I bet I could – Look – look at me now.'
> He gazed into the distance, his features composed into a simper that suggested to an impartial observer a mixture of coyness and imbecility...

Nevertheless, William *does* play the part, with disastrous results for the play, for his parents (who happen to be in the audience) and for himself, when he has to flee frantically from almost the entire school population. It is the gym mistress who in true (not so jolly) hockey-sticks fashion is in the vanguard of the pursuers, and seizes one of his ears; the art mistress grabs the other, and then the head girl clutches the scruff of his neck. The rest of his pursuers grip any portion of his anatomy that they can, and thus he is ignominiously marched off to the head mistress – and retribution.

In the same book (*William in Trouble*), Richmal has a lot of fun with another example of William (this time with the Outlaws) showing interest in a girls' school. The sight of the students of Rose Mount School dashing about a field in pursuit of a small ball and 'armed with curiously shaped sticks' intrigues the Outlaws in spite of their view that girls' activities are worthy only of derision and contempt. They struggle for some time with their feelings that this might be a game suited simply to 'inferior beings with inferior powers', but then admit that hockey has hooked them. Like the St Elphin's girls in their Warrington days, the Outlaws play a brand of the game that does not conform to orthodox rules. They 'bully' with gusto, charge, leap

27

and yell, and brandish walking-sticks (which they have 'borrowed' without permission from their long-suffering fathers) for hitting the ball and tripping each other up. 'To an impartial observer it was more suggestive of a permanent Rugger scrimmage than anything else, but it was – the Outlaws agreed emphatically – a jolly good game.'

The Lamburn girls and their parents (Clara in particular) were conscientious correspondents. Much of their communication took place on picture postcards, several of which Richmal kept, neatly bundled, until she died. The minutiae of school life come vividly across in Richmal's cards and letters to her parents:

E. Evans, Kathleen Thomas and I used to use cribs for our Latin translation (we'd had permission) and now all the class can do. Miss Flood thinks it will help them.

It was nice yesterday. I took my mack and brolly out and lay down on my mack and stuck up my brolly to keep out the sun and had a lovely read. Sometimes I do get sick of the same things day after day and week after week with nothing but a bad mark on the least exciting . . . Could you send me a white hair-ribbon for Sundays and the concert?

The following is a typical card from Richmal to Jack. It is addressed to 'Jacko' and signed 'With love, Pussy'.

How do you like this exciting picture post card? Do you remember those half hour French lessons G[wen] and I used to try to do with you? How are you getting on at school? Caught any more tadpoles? . . . Don't you wish I was at home to tease you?

Jack, in a surprisingly un-Williamesque way, on 24 August 1904 is moved to write to Richmal in French, on a picture postcard depicting Gainsborough Castle near Doncaster. He writes that this is the castle where Ivanhoe fought and put down 'the Jew', that boiling water and stones were thrown down from the castle onto enemies, and that someone (whose name is indecipherable) is expected that afternoon to play croquet. The card is signed 'Votre frère aimant – Jean'.

Edward occasionally sends Richmal a complete missive in his immaculate copperplate; more often, he pens a postscript to a communication from Clara. On one occasion Clara writes to Richmal about 'a scene at the Grammar School yesterday. Father had a fall and knocked his head against the desk, it bled profusely and the sight of the blood frightened the boys so much that about six of them fainted, one boy very badly. It was twenty minutes before they could bring him round: Father is plastered up and says he feels quite well but no doubt he will be marked by it.' She adds that Richmal shouldn't be alarmed because it isn't serious. Edward's unmistakable PS along the top of the card further reassures her that all is well, and that he merely had an accident through stepping off a form.

Clara's letters do not usually touch such high drama; more generally they are about small matters of dress – 'Ask Gwen if she knows where the sleeves of her silk frock are put' – or church and domestic doings: 'Yesterday we held our Lenten sewing meeting for the Waifs and Strays'. Clara also sends Richmal a picture postcard of Bury New Grammar School on 21 January 1904 and comments, hopefully: 'Jack seems very interested in it', adding that 'the changing rooms, electric light, all seem strange'. The tough bond of familial affection that linked the Lamburns is extremely evident in this correspondence. Richmal signs off one letter to her parents: 'I remain with everlasting love and myriads of tons of longing for you, Ray.'

Another regular correspondent with both Richmal and Gwen was Stanley Rowland, a teaching colleague of their father's at Bury Grammar School. A lifelong bachelor, he was considerably older than the two Lamburn girls, and his interest in them appears to have been avuncular. In *Anne Morrison*, Richmal almost certainly based the character of Mr Sanderson (Sandy), on him. In the book his place in Anne's early life as friend, counsellor and confidant is very similar to that occupied by Stanley in Richmal's and Gwen's. After the girls left St Elphin's, their long-standing friendship with Stanley continued, conducted largely by letters, the only snag in this being that he expected immediate replies to his lengthy epistles. Both Gwen and Richmal found difficulty in keeping up with the correspondence, and Stanley's demanding attitude became a source of great amusement to Richmal. In *Anne Morrison*, Sandy – very briefly – becomes the focus of romantic, or, rather, matrimonial, interest when as a middle-aged bachelor he proposes to Anne. Characteristically he does so by correspondence:

> My dear Anne,
> I want to ask you a question. I don't want to beat about the bush. Will you marry me? I am not a young man and I cannot offer you what a younger man might offer you, but I can offer you my devotion and protection and I would try to make you happy.
> > Yours,
> > Sandy.

Despite the parallels between Anne's fictional experiences and Richmal's real-life ones, it is unlikely that there was any suggestion of a romantic liaison between herself and Stanley Rowland, who was apparently just as fond of Gwen as he was of Richmal, and a good-humoured, cheering influence in the lives of both sisters. Their mother was upset that Richmal had based Sandy on the character of this very good family friend, but in fact Stanley didn't appear to mind, and the friendship continued without diminution.

Although much of the action in *Anne Morrison* is imaginary, Richmal lifted wholesale many St Elphin's images and events for the book. It thus provides insights into both her schoolgirl experiences and, later on, her employment there as a teacher. Anne, with her older sister Lorna, goes as a pupil to 'The Priory' (almost certainly a fictional name for the Warrington school building that housed St Elphin's until the early 1900s). Later she works as a teacher at St Catherine's, which rings with Elphinite echoes from the Darley Dale period. The in-fighting, pettiness and over-concern with themselves that characterized many of the make-believe schoolmistresses point the fact that Richmal had become acutely aware of pitfalls to avoid in her own teaching career. True to tradition, girls are 'gone on' various members of staff, some of whom encourage their attentions and deliberately make favourites. There is a 'ghost' who turns out to be a sleepwalking girl, and a secret society similar to that described in Richmal's essay about her own childhood. The vagueness about hockey regulations at St Elphin's in its early days is also reflected, as well as Richmal's response to the stimulation of the game: 'it held the thrills of victory and the sting of defeat, the glow of exercise, the excitement of the contest, the indefinable ideal of *esprit de corps*'.

The satisfactions that boarding-school life afforded Richmal socially, scholastically and in the realms of the imagination are summed up in an episode from *Anne Morrison*, which takes place in the room of Mrs Dolf, the charismatic school matron:

It was a small, low-ceilinged room with a deep fire-place and low, broad window-seat. A bright fire burnt in the grate . . .

They went over to a bookshelf and examined the books. Anne stood by Peace [a girl whom she admires].

'I'm reading *Idylls of the King*', [a favourite book of Richmal's: see pages 58 and 59] she said softly. 'Mrs. Dolf lets me read here on Sunday afternoon. Do get a book and stay too.'

Mrs. Dolf rose briskly. 'Now if you'd like to stay a minute I'll read to you . . .'.

Mrs. Dolf read the story of Sintram. It held Anne spellbound – her eyes grew bigger and bigger, her soul lost in dream – and beneath the spell a delicious consciousness of the dim beauty of the room, the flowers, the soft colourings, the firelight . . . and Peace . . .

Thus was Anne admitted into the most exclusive and secret society of the Priory.

The St Elphin's routine of lessons, games, friendships, and cosy, wet-day readings in the library laid its firm hold on Richmal. Gwen had helped to smooth her path in the early days, and bouts of homesickness were soon things of the past. Richmal became every inch the typical Edwardian schoolgirl. Yet, in spite of her satisfaction in being part of a vital, happy community, deep within her there was still sometimes the need for silence and her own company, for escape from the mainstream of school rituals and routines.

She wrote in *The Innermost Room* that a vivid imagination 'is as great a curse as it is a blessing'. Her own imaginative powers were strong, wide-ranging and of a positive nature so long as she applied them to literary creation. There were, however, some rare moments when in real-life situations Richmal's imagination succumbed to slightly morbid fears and speculations. This process might have been one facet of what she referred to as 'the enemy' in *The Innermost Room*. Escape from this enemy could often come about only by entering a secret world of pleasure, satisfaction or excitement. Richmal had learned how to retire to such worlds in her early childhood, when the attic had been her secret and special place. Secret worlds were inner as well as outer refuges, and therefore accessible to her even in the extremely communal life of school. Whenever this became (as one of her characters expresses it in *The Gypsy's Baby*) 'so noisy, one couldn't read or think', Richmal could journey outwards in her imagination to enticing locations – from Classical Greece, which endlessly intrigued her, to the 'fairy-like' fields around her home. (Fairies were as lively as ghosts in the regions of Richmal's imagination that relished the supernatural.) She could also, of course, look inwards for escape, for refuge, in one or other of her secret dreams or fantasies. In *The Innermost Room*, Bridget as a young girl has an image of herself as a series of rooms, 'beginning with an ante-room and ending with a small innermost room'. This secret-world theme is evident in almost all of Richmal's writings, from the William stories to her serious adult novels. For William and the Outlaws, the place of refuge is rather more likely to be an expedient hide-out than some more romantic setting:

> The ill-timed and tactless interference of parents had nipped in the bud many a cherished plan, and by bitter experience the Outlaws had learned that secrecy was their only protection . . .

and

> The house next door had been unoccupied for so long that William had begun to look upon its garden as his own property.

What a vision this conjures of anarchic variations on the secret-garden theme! In this context William's exploits stir the remembered experiences of every child for whom an empty, tangled garden offers enchantments that trimmed, manicured and charted plots singularly lack. For William, this particular garden – actually a waste-land of old tins, broken pots and a heterogeneous collection of rubbish – is a magnificent castle and a mighty stronghold, a place where he and his wilder flights of imagination reign supreme, secret and well hidden from adult manipulation or interference.

Richmal is at her best with the secret-world theme when William retreats into lurid daydreams inspired by a sudden infatuation for some fanciable female or other. In one instance, he falls heavily for the actress who plays the Princess Goldilocks in a pantomime to which he is taken by Robert. He becomes silent and docile at home, inwardly performing deeds of derring-do for her. His thoughts run to marriage, and the perpetual small-boy problem of extracting money from his mother, which might make this possible. When he eventually comes to close quarters with 'Princess Goldilocks', and finds her not young and sweet but 'elderly and irritable', William remains unblighted by the experience. He simply and resiliently returns his fallen idol 'in imagination' to the brigands and pirates and wild beasts from which, in his secret thoughts, he has so often rescued her.

In her adult novels, Richmal moves from the simplistic fantasies of William into secret worlds that often have a sophisticated tone and a literary slant, in *Frost at Morning*, Philip is 'a lanky over-grown boy of fourteen', with dark eyes, set above bluish shadows which give him an air of fragility. He is suffering acutely from loneliness, following his mother's death, and his father's remarriage and closeness to Philip's stepbrother, whose extroverted nature appeals more to him than Philip's reserved personality:

Philip was used to that now . . . And, till quite lately, he had been happy by himself. His imaginary world had been so real that the actual world around him mattered little. Leading his armies to victory, performing fantastic deeds of valour against his foes, circumventing the ruses of the Queen of the South, winning the love of Rosabel ... he could give a hundred twists to the familiar story. Then gradually he had lost interest in the saga and, instead, had begun to identify himself with the hero of every story he read. As Kenneth of Scotland, he went to the Holy Land in disguise to fight for Richard Coeur de Lion; as Hereward the Wake, he led his outlaws and defied the tyrant; as Odysseus, he evaded the wiles of Circe ... and freed her victims.

A feature of the juvenile refuge, secret place or activity recognized by Richmal is that generally grown-ups are completely unaware of it. For example, one of the Outlaws' shows is to take place in William's bedroom, when his mother is out and his father expected to be dead to the world in an after-lunch doze on the library sofa. The show is widely advertised amongst the neighbourhood children under orders of dire secrecy. Horrible threats of the vengeance that William and co. will wreak on them if the secret is disclosed to grown-ups keep many of the children awake at nights. And no word leaks out to parental ears.

Richmal's own secret worlds, nurtured in her schooldays, were eventually to provide comic or poignant material for her books. At the factual level, her days at the Clergy Daughters' School brought the final fulfilment of distinguished results in the Cambridge University Higher Local Examinations, and a founder's entrance scholarship to Royal Holloway College. Her schooldays were over, although her relationship with St Elphin's was not to be entirely severed.

CHAPTER 3

STUDENT AND SUFFRAGIST

"Need I have William?" she pleaded pitifully. "He's so awful."

Richmal had little difficulty in choosing a profession to train for.
Much as she enjoyed writing, she decided (with prudent
prompting from her parents) to follow in Edward's footsteps
and become a teacher. St Elphin's offered its older students
instruction and practice in teaching methods as well as purely
academic studies, which is doubtless one reason why Richmal
remained there for so long (ten years in all). In 1911 she
acquitted herself so well in the Cambridge Higher Local
Examinations that she could have had a place at Newnham.
Earlier, however, she had been awarded an open entrance
scholarship, of £60 per year, to Royal Holloway College, which
she had already accepted.

Royal Holloway College, although part of London

University, was (and is) situated at Egham (Englefield Green) in Surrey, so Richmal's move south to commence her college career brought her firmly into the Home Counties stockbroker belt that was eventually to become the setting for William's notorious exploits. There was always a vagueness in the stories about the exact location of William's village, which was never given even a fictional name. In a letter to Gerry Allison (quoted in the 1962 *Collectors' Digest Annual*) Richmal Crompton commented: 'I have received a careful plan of it drawn by a young reader, from the various stories, but in actual fact I am afraid that I just set down people and houses in places where I want them for the particular story I am writing. The village in which William lives is entirely imaginary ... a small country village in Kent – or perhaps Surrey or Sussex, within easy reach of London...'

William enthusiasts from areas far removed from London sometimes dispute that the Brown family's village is sited within commuting distance of the capital. But London is occasionally mentioned in the saga, and Richmal once wrote that Mr Brown was probably running a small family business in the City, such as the making of leather handbags or some similar enterprise. A surprising choice, one feels, for the work of William's father. Everything about his habits (commuting to town on respectably timed trains, perpetual preoccupation with newspapers and financial matters) and his appearance (bowler-hatted and pin-stripe-suited) suggests the Stock Exchange or, at any rate, a career in accountancy, rather than one in the world of women's fashion accessories.

Clara and Edward were proud of both their daughters, whose early promise of academic distinction seemed set to be fulfilled. Jack, however, was still not carving an academic niche for himself at Bury Grammar School, and Edward, reluctantly but remorselessly, was being forced into acceptance of the fact that his only son would never take up the career in the Church that his parents had planned for him. The divergence of Jack's own and his father's vicarious ambitions provided a stimulus for incidents in several of Richmal's adult novels. Paul confides to his sister, in *Anne Morrison*, that he can't possibly 'be a parson' because he yearns to travel – 'I want some adventure'. And in

The Innermost Room Derek tells his sister, Bridget, of his conviction 'that he could never make good in England, and that he could do so abroad'. This was exactly Jack Lamburn's situation, and when Richmal went to Royal Holloway in the October of 1911 she knew that Jack and his father were almost on a collision course as far as the former's career prospects were concerned. (Jack was later to find the adventure that he craved when he joined the Rhodesian Mounted Police; he thus embraced a life of action of which William, his fictional counterpart, would have approved.)

University life offered everything that Richmal hoped for: "long country walks, interminable discussions, lectures that seemed to open doors revealing golden vistas beyond them, freedom, friendship, adventure" (*The Innermost Room*). She distinguished herself as a scholar, became a keen sportswoman, and made the most of the social scene. In 1911/12 she became the senior first-year student; she gained a university open classical scholarship for one year in 1912, and in 1914, the college's Driver Scholarship in Classics. So Richmal's brains were already bringing her financial rewards – something that must have given her great satisfaction, even though she relished learning for its own sake. Higher educational opportunities and worthwhile careers for girls were still extremely sparse in the period before the Great War, but Richmal quickly proved that she would have no difficulty in supporting herself.

She remained at Royal Holloway until October 1914, when she obtained her BA degree in classics, with second class honours, 'being the best candidate of her year' (according to a testimonial from Margaret E. J. Taylor, MA, who was the senior staff tutor in classics at the college).* There is no doubt that her tutors thought highly of her. Miss Taylor mentions her vigour, and 'mastery of language' (which no one ever then predicted would be lavished on literature like the William stories). The same tutor was also impressed by the ease and fluency of Richmal's Latin and Greek translation, her 'useful command of

* Richmal Ashbee comments that the degree examinations were taken in October, which is why, 'despite coming top of the University, she only achieved a 2.1 and not a 1st. Nobody's mind was properly on his/her studies in October 1914' (when, of course, the First World War had recently started).

vocabulary and idiom' and the fact that 'her Latin prose was often markedly good in style and phrasing'. Richmal's enjoyment of Latin and Greek contrasts sharply with William's rejection of any language other than his own:

> '. . . if they wanter talk to me they can learn English. English's easy to talk. It's *silly* havin' other langwidges. I don't see why other countries shun't learn English 'stead of us learnin' other langwidges with no *sense* in 'em. English's *sense*.

Another of Richmal's tutors, A. Margaret Ramsey, lecturer in classics, admired her 'quickness and facility of apprehension', and her ability to express herself 'well and fluently in essay-writing and translation into English'. Richmal was Miss Ramsey's pupil not only in Latin and Greek but in ancient and Roman history – subjects, of course, that were anathema to William, although he is occasionally inspired with enthusiasm for archaeological excavation. His slender sense of history usually asserts itself only when he is putting on some sort of performance in order to raise funds. In his opinion, meticulous research into any period is pure irrelevance, for he is convinced that anyone can 'make up history people's clothes' for they 'jus' wore tablecloths and long stockings and funny things on their heads'.

William not only confuses tablecloths with togas, but wrecks a whole lecture by a distinguished archaeological professor on the subject of Roman excavations. Quite unintentionally the Outlaws switch the lecturer's collection of precious props (fragments of vases, jewellery, sandal buckles, etc.) for a bizarre assortment of their own and their families' things (a rusting toasting-fork, an old sardine tin, and so on). When the very short-sighted professor waxes lyrical about the taste and workmanship of an exquisite statuette, his surprised assistant finds himself holding up for the audience's inspection a battered and mothy toy goose that belongs to Henry's baby sister. The hideous face of the goose upon its wobbly neck leers horribly at the audience while the professor continues to enthuse about the exhibit's grace of posture and dignity of outline.

Archaeological digs interested Richmal from her college days and throughout her life; on several occasions she made an excavation the vehicle for some of William's colourful and comic efforts to be helpful. He also tramples frequently on the Glory that was Greece (which so much intrigued Richmal). In a holiday episode William and Ginger make off in a boat and think they've come to some strange foreign land. The 'savages' they see turn out to be members of the New School of Greek Dancing, who carry out their cavortings a few miles away from the hotel where William's and Ginger's families are staying:

> Weedy males and aesthetic-looking females dressed in abbreviated tunics with sandals on their feet and fillets round their hair, mostly wearing spectacles, ran and sprang and leapt and gambolled and struck angular attitudes at the shrill command of the instructress and the somewhat unmusical efforts of the (very) amateur flute player.

At Royal Holloway, Richmal continued to play hockey and tennis, and she took up rowing. The following description was written by a student whose college days just overlapped with Richmal's:

> ... the river ... played a great part in our lives and was a source of infinite refreshment to many of us. No student was allowed to go on the river until she had swum three lengths of the Swimming Bath comfortably. Boats containing students had to have a captain and either two efficients or one efficient and two moderates, and a list of crews had to be given in the night before. (W. E. Delp, *Royal Holloway College 1908–1914*)

No record exists of whether Richmal was an 'efficient' or a 'moderate'.

A feature of life at Royal Holloway was the College picnic which took place towards the end of every summer term, and which 'ended with boats linked together gliding gently downstream to the singing of folk-songs, College songs or whatever'.

While she was at college, Richmal staunchly upheld the Anglicanism in which she had been brought up. Her days began with an 8 a.m. service in the chapel, which was always sung.

(This service was compulsory except where students' parents had expressed objections.) There were plenty of other opportunities for worship: the principal conducted a daily evening service in the chapel, and an extra Church of England service was provided every Sunday morning. As well as public devotions, there was the customary college emphasis on debates and discussions about religion and metaphysics. Richmal's classics tutor, Margaret Taylor (nicknamed Cato), seemed to be a protagonist in this field, if a somewhat formidable one. W. E. Delp comments that, at a discussion group on Christian apologetics, Miss Taylor rounded on a student: 'Now . . . if you still can't accept the existence of God, I think we shall have to part company for the time being.'

Margaret Taylor was one of the many strong-minded women whom Richmal was to encounter during the course of her college and teaching life. She was, apparently, a tough fighter for causes that she supported, such as careers for women in the Church, and women's suffrage. We have no evidence that Richmal embraced the first of these causes, but she was certainly an active (though never a militant) suffragist. (When discussing the campaign for the vote in later years, she firmly made the distinction between suffragists and suffragettes.) At Royal Holloway, she supported meetings, distributed leaflets, and acted as a teller at elections and debates on women's suffrage. There are, however, only pale echoes in her writing of this special interest, or even of feminism in general:

> Anne Morrison was no feminist at this stage. Boys were the Superior Sex, and praise from Paul meant more than praise from Lorna or Cathy would have done.

Of course, by the time Richmal's novels began to be published, middle-class and professional women had already wrested the vote from war-weary male politicians, who, because of women's impressive contribution to the war effort, could no longer insist on their total passivity and domestic orientation. Had William come upon the literary scene a few years earlier, Richmal would surely have sent up the more extreme activities of the militant suffragettes by letting her anarchic anti-hero loose on them.

Denied such opportunities by the time-scale of the women's suffrage campaign, she contented herself instead with just an occasional side-swipe at female chauvinists. In *William the Good* (1928), the ladies of yet another high-faluting literary society that has sprung up in the village are determined to keep their membership 'select', and to confine entry to their own sex. Their view, as a Miss Featherstone voices it, is that 'as soon as you begin to have men in a thing, it complicates it at once. I've often noticed it. There's something *restless* about men. And they aren't literary. It's no good pretending they are.' William indisputably typifies the 'restless', non-literary male, and needless to say he totally disrupts one of the society's most precious projects. Although William's path is occasionally crossed by some perfectly frightful harridans, he generally manages to cut them down to size.

It is interesting that in Richmal's adult novels, feminism – as fact or aspiration – usually crops up in a college context. This is probably because it was only at this time in her own life that she felt seriously involved in feminist issues. Later on, in common with many women who have extremely successful careers, Richmal seems to have considered feminist principles as something to take for granted rather than something to campaign for.

Once again it is in *The Innermost Room* and *Anne Morrison* that Richmal discusses a subject that is of strong interest to her. In the former, Bridget is still reserved and rather oversensitive. She has nevertheless matured sufficiently to be considered as no longer 'queer' but, in the most wholesome sense, to be just one of the girls in the college chummery. Her tutor is the 'small precise and elderly Miss Gill . . . She was an intense feminist, and she considered that one of her duties in life was to rend the veils of ignorance from the eyes of the young.' Bridget, we should remember, has always spent a lot of her time and energy clinging on to any kind of veil which shields her from that mysterious 'more sinister than death' inner and outer 'enemy' that crops up in so many guises, from drunkenness to dancing women, before Bridget finally faces it in its unadulterated and naked form (see page 131). Miss Gill's fearfully aggressive feminism takes the form of exorcizing from her students what she calls 'false

41

modesty': 'Her translations of certain portions of the classics would have made a Mormon blush.' Miss Gill, who takes a fancy to Bridget, hints darkly at the social evils that lie in wait for underpaid working women, who are told by their exploitive employers, 'No-one expects you to live on that. You have your nights . . .' (Bridget guesses that this means 'something horrid', but is too innocent to understand what Miss Gill is referring to.)

The first feminist encountered by Bridget is pretty frightful, and Anne Morrison also, when she is at college, finds some aspects of the women's suffrage movement distinctly disturbing. She meets the eloquent but fanatical Sylvia, who is an old schoolmate. Sylvia urges her to join the suffragists; she sees votes for women as the panacea for such social ills as the sweated labour of women and young girls. She tells Anne that she doesn't expect her to start campaigning until after her finals, and then that she need only, as a beginning, lobby MPs in the streets or from the Ladies' Gallery of the House: 'I won't ask you to burn a church or anything . . . though, if that frightens 'em, I'd burn down every church in England.' Strong sentiments for a character created by a clergy daughter – but Sylvia has made terrible sacrifices for the cause, suffering imprisonment and forced feeding – 'Can you see these scars? They used broken saucers to force our lips open' – and the loss of a fiancé who finds all this militancy a bit much.

Anne feels terribly responsible for her exploited sisters-under-the-skin, but, being more timid by nature than Sylvia, she undergoes torments in her imagination as she contemplates the consequences of pitting her puny strength against the Establishment. However, before 'that call to Service and Sacrifice to which youth so readily responds' finally claims her, the 1914–18 war begins – and she learns, with inexpressible relief, that 'the militants have declared a truce'.

In a sense Richmal seems to play devil's advocate and frequently to take an anti-feminist narrative view. In *The Wildings*, when Clare and Cedric Farrar are falling in love with each other, Clare is very much the little woman, and he the all-providing man of the world of the type that Richmal mocks in the William books:

She saw him turn aside from her, and the thought that she might have offended him was unbearable ... 'Is it – is it awfully hard to learn to drive a car?' she said ...

He smiled down at her.

'No, quite easy. I'll teach you one day.'

Radiant happiness again flooded her ... He wasn't annoyed ... It was all right.

'I've got to go to Russia next month ... I'll bring you back a nice mug with "A Present from Russia for a Good Girl" on it, shall I?'

The dimples – the adorable smile.

'Oh do – I would love it.'

'You'd have to earn it, you know, by writing to me.

They'll tell you how many stamps to put on at the post office ...'

Richmal's adult novels suggest that in her view being attractive to men involved women in accepting the traditional role of vacuous passivity: Richmal, for example, is closer in personality to David Wilding's artistic and intelligent wife, Hero – yet narratively she does little to support her. Hero never really achieves the love and comradeship from her husband that she deserves. She reflects bitterly that although Clare is 'timid, yielding, not particularly intellectual or particularly well educated', it is women like her whom 'men always loved and always would love most passionately'.

Fictional descriptions of college life in *The Innermost Room* and *Anne Morrison* – 'work and friendship, both such very, very pleasant things' – were strongly influenced by Richmal's three years at Royal Holloway College. Her zest for life and her ready but genial wit attracted many people to her, and with two especially close friends from these student days, Gladys Allan and Elsie Brown (later Wilmore), she maintained extremely long-standing relationships. She and Elsie went on several foreign holidays together (see page 112). Gladys was an out-spoken Scot, whose robustness appealed to Richmal.

However, when Gladys wrote a long diary of her years at college, on 'Dear Diary' lines, and invited Richmal's comments on this, Richmal actually took a dim view of it, but was too kind to echo Gladys's forthrightness in expressing this opinion. Gladys also had a habit at Christmas time of sending to friends the presents that she had received during the previous festive season. The complications that ensued from this practice almost certainly inspired a very entertaining episode in Richmal's *Enter – Patricia* (1927), when the heroine's husband, misunderstanding a domestic instruction, inadvertently sends to several friends and relatives the presents which they have previously given to Patricia and himself.

Despite the fulfilments of her social life at college, Richmal frequently succumbed to the sense of inadequacy that is so often associated with growing up. She harnesses this in *The Innermost Room* to express Bridget's fears and uncertainties: 'Youth wants a calm and safe stream' but 'it was more like the beginning of a wood ... and there were things behind the trees that might pounce out at you suddenly ... things one heard, things one saw. And really right down at the bottom, youth was frightened – even in the patches of sunshine ... frightened of what lay before...'

Years later (in 1966) Richmal expressed her sense of the vulnerability of youth in a letter to Joan Braunholtz (an ex-pupil who became a lifelong friend):

> Oddly, I've been reading Tolstoy's *Childhood, Boyhood and Youth* too. It's fascinating, isn't it? I think that his descriptions of adolescence are terrifyingly true – the self-consciousness, the hot humiliations, the ... showing off and self-dramatization, the fantastic imaginary scenes one puts oneself through, and beneath it all the horrible uncertainty and self-loathing, mixed with ineffable conceit. I often feel glad I've left youth behind – it's an over-rated time of life.

Strange words from one who wrote with such vigour and exhilaration about the aspirations of childhood!

Most of Richmal's time at Royal Holloway, however, passed happily. The college community was small and intimate (about 150 students) when she joined it, and there were few barriers between staff and students. High spots were the annual garden parties, which were frequently attended by royal personages, and which were further distinguished by 'mountains of strawberries and rivers of cream', with a brass band playing on the terrace while everyone tucked in. The college building was less than lovely; its flaming red bricks were said to scorch the eye. Happily, however, the extensive grounds mellowed it – smooth and spacious lawns, a great monkey-puzzle tree whose lower branches swept the ground, and plentiful azaleas and rhododendrons softened the brash façade.

There was a great deal of interest in drama, and Richmal's contributions to theatricals were enthusiastic, and the subject of warm appreciation in a testimonial from Margaret Taylor: '[She] has contributed to the general amusement by her acting and by her facility in producing occasional verses.' Richmal, as well as being active in the college dramatic presentations, became secretary to its classical club. She was also librarian for the Christian Union from 1912 to 1913, and then its treasurer until 1914.

Regular college meetings took place, to discuss any problems that might arise from internal and external student policy. Royal Holloway College, out at Egham, was somewhat divorced from the main body of London University: public transport to the city, which Richmal and her colleagues would have had to use, consisted of only a few trains (none of which was late enough to allow evening theatre visits, although matinées were possible), and occasional buses to Staines or Windsor. There were also horse-cabs, but for the most part the girls travelled on foot or by bicycle – which didn't worry the athletic Richmal.

Because the college was so tucked away, there were occasional misapprehensions about its true function. Its founder was the Holloway of Holloway's pills, and as well as building the college he endowed a 'lunatic asylum'.* One day a party of American tourists stopped at the entrance to the college, and were told by their guide that this was the asylum. The college Principal, who was then entering the gates, corrected this statement, only to hear one of the Americans (still convinced that the college was a mental home) say to another member of the party: 'That's the way it takes her, poor dear!'

---

* It is thus described in *Sixty Odd Years*, by Thomas Rhodes Disher (1954) from which this anecdote has been taken.

During Richmal's period at Royal Holloway, the Principal was Miss Ellen C. Higgins, who presided competently and graciously over public events, and was known to her students as 'The Chief'. She was a determined Scotswoman who still adhered to the tailor-made ground-length 'costumes' that had been the typical garb of women teachers during the previous decade. Apparently she respected students who showed a strong measure of spirit and independence, but was apt to 'shatter the hypersensitive'. She put her battling instincts to good use, however, struggling tirelessly and successfully for the standing of Royal Holloway College within the University.

Richmal's college years came to an end in October 1914, after that serene summer that can be seen, with hindsight, as the calm before the calamitous storm which broke upon the world in August, and was to engulf it through four agonizing years.

CHAPTER 4

TEACHING THEM MORE THAN LATIN

"Do you never listen to a word I say?" asked the history master.

Richmal left Royal Holloway College to return to St Elphin's as classics mistress in the autumn term of 1914. Her world had been a scholastic one since 1901, when she had first gone to St Elphin's as a schoolgirl, and it seemed likely that for many more years she would remain dedicated to teaching and study. Gwen had opted for more variety in her career. She obtained her London University degree in Latin, French and Maths (the same subjects that her father took) by studying at home and attending some lectures at Manchester University. She worked for a short period as a pupil teacher at St Elphin's, and then took a secretarial course, and began to look for congenial work. Staying periodically with a cousin in London, she had already spent some time in the south, and in the summer of 1914 she was interviewed for a secretarial job by Thomas Rhodes Disher, a successful entrepreneur with a finger in many business pies. Disher was a man with strong convictions and an equally vigorous way of expressing these. He comments in his autobiographical book *Sixty Odd Years* (1954) that he advertised for a secretary who should be a non-smoker and a total abstainer. When Gwen (who didn't exactly follow this abstemious regime) came for her interview, he took her to tea at his parents' home, and then to the theatre to see *Potash and Perlmutter*. After this, he escorted her to Euston for the northern night train, and she went home to Bury.

Gwen started work as his secretary in August, the month that marked the commencement of the Great War. Obviously, Disher had almost immediately decided that his interest in Gwen was more than a strictly business one. He visited the Lamburns in Bury for a weekend later in August, when Richmal was also there. Disher made an extremely favourable impression upon Edward and Clara – but not on Richmal. She never took to him, in spite of the fact that he considerably admired her prowess in both teaching and writing. In his autobiography he records that one of his guests, the sales manager of an extremely large company, spoke at the dinner-table of sending his two daughters to St Elphin's because his elder girl wanted a scholarship to Oxford, and he had heard of the excellent reputation of the school's senior classics mistress. Disher was able to point out that the lady in question (Richmal, of course) was at that moment seated at his side. The sales manager's daughters *did* go to St Elphin's, and happily the girl who had set her heart on Oxford won the desired scholarship under Richmal's tutelage.

Edward Lamburn, generous-natured but conventional, was probably surprised when, a few weeks after meeting Disher, he was asked by telegram for Gwen's hand in marriage: 'May I have your baa-lamb for keeps?' Parental consent was given, and Gwen married Thomas Disher in October 1914 at St Paul's in Onslow Square, London.

Richmal's specific thoughts on this occasion are not recorded, but, even though she didn't regard Thomas as a suitable husband for Gwen, she remained psychologically close to her sister, and considered the possibilities of moving to London to be physically near her. Such plans, however, could only be thought of as belonging to the future. She had made a promise to Miss Margaret Flood (who became the head of St Elphin's in 1910) to teach there for two or three years after she had graduated. Also, she felt bound to remain fairly near to Clara and Edward, as Jack had sailed far away from them in 1913 when he had finally turned his back on the possibility of a Church or an academic career, and joined the Rhodesian Mounted Police. Because of the outbreak of war, he was unable to come home for several years, although he would have liked to be released from his Rhodesian duties in order to serve on the Western Front.

The Lamburn family suffered a more permanent loss in 1915, when Edward, in hospital for a minor operation, surprisingly and tragically died under anaesthetic. Clara had no desire to rattle around like a lone pea in the very large pod of the Malvern Villas house, so, with Richmal living in at St Elphin's, Gwen and Thomas invited Clara to live with them. The Bury house was given up and Clara joined the Dishers, who first lived in a flat in Camberwell Road and then in another south-east London home. This was 147 Denmark Hill, a rather grand house which Disher describes as having a full carriage sweep and a large garden with tennis court, hot-house and a private lane to Denmark Hill Station.

Richmal enjoyed teaching at St Elphin's, in the environment which had so much influenced her girlhood and adolescence. Miss Flood wrote in 1917 of her 'very high opinion of Miss Lamburn's classical abilities and of her character'. She considered her method of teaching 'very sound' and that she was a good influence on the school and 'a most pleasant colleague'.

Possibly Richmal's feelings about Miss Flood were rather less enthusiastic; when *Anne Morrison* was published in 1925, Miss Flood was so shocked and hurt by its critical references to a headmistress (who she considered was based upon herself) that she banned the book from St Elphin's. (It is interesting that Richmal should have suffered a literary ban early in her writing career, as well as towards its end when one or two misguided librarians decided to remove the William books from their shelves. This, presumably, was because William's background was felt to be too middle-class and outdated for the average child reader of the late 1960s – a view that seems hardly tenable in the light of the tremendous success with children that the 1980s reprints of the books have had.)

Earlier, Richmal's attitude to Margaret Flood seems to have been very cordial. When she and Gwen were schoolgirls at Warrington, they were once taken on holiday by her to the Lake District. And, later on, when Richmal was working for her entrance scholarship to Royal Holloway College, she had much appreciated Miss Flood's coaching.

Anne Morrison describes the life and inmates of two residential girls' schools, one which Anne attended as a pupil and one at which she taught after graduating from college. Several former St Elphinites believed that these establishments were based on their old school, and wondered whether Miss Rose, the rather vain and self-opinionated headmistress of the fictional St Catherine's, might have been inspired by Miss Flood. Miss Rose has an erratic approach to discipline and makes favourites of girls and teachers who pander to her vanity; she has 'a fiendish temper', and is self-indulgent to the extent of urging patriotic wartime economies on others whilst remaining greedy herself. Worst of all, perhaps, she has regular attacks of hysterics – hardly in the tradition of the stiff-upper-lip girls' school teacher. Certainly this particular fictional headmistress is drawn acerbically – but it should be remembered that Richmal's wit was rarely pitted against real-life personalities. Almost everyone who knew her well and enjoyed her lively anecdotes has commented on the unmalicious quality of her humour. However, the unfortunate Miss Flood remained convinced that Miss Rose was the parodied immortalization in literature of herself. The final straw (according to Lady Sybil Osmond, a former St Elphinite who is now on its board of governors) must have been Richmal's description of the headmistress trying hard (but unsuccessfully) to attract the attentions of a visiting male lecturer.

Though Miss Rose was now forty years old the general opinion of the staff was that she had 'not given up hope yet' . . .

. . . Mr Plumb came to lecture the week after half term. He was about fifty – very thin and tall and elegant, with grey hair and a charming smile . . . Miss Rose wore a new evening dress and did her hair in a new style which made her look much younger. She was flushed and very pretty. She was in excellent spirits all day, coquettishly young in manner and as excited as a child . . .

Miss Rose listened brightly and intelligently to the lecture from an arm-chair in the front row, holding the 'baby of the school' on her knee . . . [she] was a little girl with golden curls and very blue eyes, and Miss Rose considered, not unreasonably, that they made a pretty picture . . .

It seems unlikely that Richmal clashed overtly with Miss Flood when she taught at St Elphin's from 1914 to 1917, for when she left her headmistress provided her with a generous and glowing testimonial.

It is satisfying to be able to record that these two distinguished ladies from St Elphin's were, much later in life, to be reconciled. Lady Sybil Osmond remained friendly with them both and, in the 1950s, determined to heal the breach. Miss Flood was then staying with her, at her Beckenham house, which was not very far from Richmal's home (then at Chislehurst in Kent). Richmal accepted an invitation to tea, and to meet again the now retired Margaret Flood. Lady Sybil comments that at first things seemed to go terribly badly. 'Ray sat on one of the new garden chairs on the terrace, and it collapsed.' Her hostess was extremely concerned, but 'Ray was very nice about it, and the incident broke the ice between Miss Flood and herself. Each found the other an interesting and outstanding person – and they agreed to let bygones be bygones.' Lady Sybil, by the way, says she was devoted to Miss Flood, who was 'a great headmistress'.

Once Clara had gone to live with Gwen, Richmal made up her mind to find teaching work in or near London in order to be near her mother and sister. And there was a further emotional pull to London in the shape of the new baby, Thomas Edward Lamburn, who had been born to the Dishers in the July of 1915. (Tommy's mischievous boyhood was to provide his aunt with further ideas and sources of inspiration for William's unending string of exploits.) Richmal applied, and was accepted, for the post of classics mistress at Bromley High School (a Girls' Public

Day School Trust establishment) in one of the greener and more pleasant suburbs of London, in the county of Kent.

The High School was already outgrowing its premises when Richmal joined the staff.* In 1917 it stood in Elmfield Road, one of Bromley's select residential areas, just off its busy High Street, and near to Bromley South station which links the suburb with central London (Victoria) in one direction and the Kent and Sussex coast in the other. Richmal bought a house in Cherry Orchard Road, three and a half miles away from the school, in the then almost rustic district known as Bromley Common. She enjoyed cycling, and went to work each day by bicycle. As well as this regular quota of exercise, she continued sometimes to play hockey in the staff versus girls matches which the school encouraged.

Clara left the Dishers to come to Cherry Orchard Road, happy to put her considerable housekeeping skills into action once again. She managed domestic matters, leaving Richmal free to concentrate on teaching – and on writing. It is no cliché to say that Richmal was a dedicated teacher; nevertheless, she also found time to write fiction, particularly in the form of short stories. In 1917 the market for these was vast. Many weekly and monthly magazines existed – *Pearson's*, the *Strand*, the *Happy*, the *Sunny*, the *Quiver*, etc. – which specialized in fiction and, apart from one or two serials, concentrated on the type of pithy and well constructed short complete story that was to become Richmal's forte. Her first tale to be published appeared in a 1918 issue of the misleadingly named *Girl's Own Paper* (which at that time, far from appealing to girls, was very much a women's paper). Called (perhaps with Gwen's small son in mind) 'Thomas', and subtitled 'A Little Boy Who Would Grow Up', this story can be seen as a bland forerunner of the William adventures, and it incorporates several of the themes that Richmal was to use repeatedly, with ever-increasing skill.

It is a rite of passage episode, dealing with a small boy's revolt against adult authority, and with a boyhood friendship. Thomas is one of those pretty smock-and-romper-clad curly-headed

---

* The school expanded by taking over other houses in Elmfield Road, until the beginning of 1981, when it moved to new purpose-built premises in Blackbrook Lane, Bickley, Kent.

little boys whom one sees illustrated in popular magazines of the 1910s and 1920s, but whose style of dress (fortunately) faded out completely at some time during the less sentimental 1930s. (Incidentally the 'mummy's little darling' archetype was to become a symbol for retrogressive attitudes towards childhood in Richmal's later stories. Whenever William of the spiky hair and scruffy clothes finds himself up against a satin- or sailor-suited boy with 'Bubbles'-like golden curls, the leader of the Outlaws always, and gratifyingly, gets the better of him.)

Strangely, it is another boy called William who jolts the neat and sweet seven-year-old Thomas away from his mother's apron strings and into the world of real and robust boyhood. Thomas and William are close friends and, at the beginning of the story, they are both adorned with riotous curls and smocks and sandals. William is the first to revolt – he turns up at school 'with a conscious swagger and a superior smile . . . with his hair cut close to his head and all his . . . curls gone'. He also sports a sensible suit, 'turned down stockings' (socks) and proper shoes, and has the 'air of a finished man-about-town'.

Thomas yearns to undergo a similar transformation, but is deterred by the knowledge that his mother – 'What should I do without my curly-headed baby?' – likes him as he is. William in his new and manly guise taunts Thomas, and goads him into a fight, which Thomas rather surprisingly wins. As spoils of victory he claims one of William's new 'grown-up' suits, and demands a very basic scissor haircut from his vanquished chum. Thus transformed, and trembling with apprehension, he prepares to meet his mother, afraid that she will reject her new-look son. She doesn't, of course:

> she looked at the unevenly-cropped head, the smeared little face with the black swollen eye, and, lastly the brand new flannel suit . . . she smiled with eyes that were rather misty. 'Oh, I love my grown-up son,' she said gravely, 'just as much as I ever loved my baby boy.' Thomas sighed a sigh of relief, and a seraphic all-embracing smile of happiness spread over his little face as he nestled down into the familiar shelter of her arms.

Doubtless William Brown (whom one is tempted to call the *real* William) would have found all this 'sicknin' – but it is a step in the right direction for Richmal, launching her as a writer of fiction *for* adults *about* children. Soon afterwards, of course, this was to be the format for the William stories too. The editors and readers of the *Girl's Own Paper* seem to have responded warmly to 'Thomas', for it was quickly followed up by another, and a more serious, story entitled 'Mrs Tempest; And the Children She Tried to Mother'. (Mrs Tempest is a good-hearted second wife, whose kindness is constantly flung in her teeth by the ungrateful offspring of her husband's first marriage.)

These early published stories appeared with the Richmal Crompton byline. The High School (Girls' Public Day School Trust) had a rule that their staff should have no other employment without the Headmistress's express permission. Richmal was not sure whether her free-lance writing counted as 'other employment', but played for safety by not using her full name, rather than take the alternative and embarrassing course of asking permission. She forgot, however, that the annual index to *Punch* used proper names, not noms de plume. Miss Hodge, the Head, saw this and sent for Richmal, who very nervously went to see her. She was greeted with an excited 'My dear, why didn't you tell me?' Gradually after this the identity of the author of the William stories leaked out to the school, but, with the need for concealment over, Richmal still retained the pen-name.

(Miriam Place, a former Bromley High School pupil, recollects how surprised she was when, in the early 1920s, a friend showed her *Just – William*, and told her that 'Lambie', as Richmal was called by her girls, wrote it.) Miss Place remembers her as a handsome, charismatic and stimulating teacher, and so too do Joan Braunholtz (née Raymont) and Audrey Carr. Miriam Place speaks of Richmal's light-brown hair – 'lots of it' – which was always smartly twirled into buns, plaits or "headphones" '. Joan Braunholtz refers to her 'lively blue eyes,* and corn-coloured hair', and her 'neat navy blue dress' enlivened by a string of white beads. Every one of her students seems to have appreciated the exuberant sense of humour that came

* Richmal Ashbee remembers her aunt as having 'hazelly-grey' eyes.

across in Richmal's teaching. 'She was most inspiring and enthusiastic – laughter and fun were the essential ingredients of the lessons' (Joan Braunholtz). Writing in the Bromley High School magazine (1968–9) after Richmal's death, Audrey Carr says that 'Miss Lamburn was always tolerant and patient, and her keen sense of humour was a great help; amusing stories, atrocious puns, silly jokes, impressed rules and vocabulary on our minds where learning by rote would have failed.'

Joan Braunholtz comments: '. . . of course we girls had "crushes" on her. One girl used to bring a single rose, and place it on her desk before she came in'. It is not surprising that a young, pretty and vivacious teacher should inspire crushes in her adolescent pupils, but what is unusual is that, so many decades later, she is still remembered by mature and intelligent women in such glowing terms. There is no doubt that she had what one of them has termed 'a magnetic presence'. But she could be tough too, 'downright . . . standing no nonsense . . . and quite sharp with anyone who "tried it on" '.

It is interesting to see how Richmal, having been on the receiving end of youthful crushes, writes about the infatuation which William develops for one of his teachers. The episode begins with William feeling deeply bored by the arithmetical problem that Miss Drew is trying to explain to him. Richmal, in ironical mood, comments that Miss Drew is also bored, although, unlike William, she tries to hide the fact. However, as 'teaching on a hot afternoon is rather trying', Miss Drew cuts off in full flood William's eloquent protestations about arithmetic not making sense, and tells him to stay in after school for further explanations. It is then that, while she bends over her desk, the sun streams in through the window and illuminates the golden curls in the nape of her neck:

> There was a faint perfume about her, and William the devil-may-care-pirate and robber-chief, the stern despiser of all things effeminate, felt the first dart of the malicious blind god.

Desperate to please his teacher, he says that he now 'unnerstands' the problems with which they have been grappling. She points out wearily that he'd have found it easier if he hadn't played with dead lizards all the time when he should have been concentrating in class, and, we are told, 'He went home her devoted slave'!

Surprisingly, Richmal never wrote the authentic girls' school story which she forecast would one day be published with a day-school setting. Her teaching experiences at Bromley High School gave her ideal material to tackle this theme, but, sadly, she never undertook it in depth, although several of her novels include tantalising snatches of schoolgirlish action and dialogue, like the following from *Frost at Morning*:

A schoolgirl, blonde and massive, passed the seat with a companion who was obviously an earnest copy of her friend.

'I had it out with her in the dorm. this morning,' the massive one was saying in a ringing, authoritative voice.

'I said, "Look here, Honor, we don't want to have the same trouble over the hockey next term that we've had over the cricket. Are you going to pull your weight with the team or aren't you? That's the question." '

Although she never wrote a schoolgirl story, Richmal *did* make several attempts at producing a leading girl character with vitality and appeal that might be similar to William's. She didn't succeed, partly because their over-domestic settings proved their undoing. Little Veronica in *Kathleen and I, and, of Course, Veronica* (1926) lacks conviction, and the determinedly bouncy heroines of *Enter – Patricia* (1927), and *Felicity Stands By* (1928) are stereotyped bright young things rather than vigorously addictive juveniles.

Kathleen and I, and, of Course, Veronica is a collection of short stories about a young couple and their mischievous small daughter, Veronica, who is, unfortunately, less engaging than the narrative voice tries to persuade us that she is, and who comes across as only a partly-cooked 'cutie-pie' – a Violet Elizabeth stripped of her physical frills and her psychological flounces.

There is a touch of coyness in the overall mood of *Felicity Stands By*. The heroine is sixteen when the book begins. It is indicated that she has been the tearaway of the elite boarding-school which she has just left. She is supposed to continue her studies 'quietly at home ... until she comes out' – but she has other ideas. Richmal has other ideas about her too. But she doesn't quite make up her mind how Felicity can combine the romantic appeal of someone who looks like a 'stained glass window Saint of the Middle Ages', and who is 'light as thistle-down and as graceful as a silver birch', with the hard-hitting, straight-from-the-shoulder honesty that she is supposed to embody. Felicity *does* have possibilities, however, and it is a pity that Richmal didn't persist with her, tone down her 'rich, red-gold, curly thick' hair and her 'speedwell blue eyes,' to concentrate on her William-like capacity for debunking pretentious and hypocritical adults. If Richmal had allowed Felicity to function in the boarding-school setting that she is extracted from so early in the book, Felicity might have become a tremendous character. As it is, in age and by inclination she is accessible to adult experiences but incapable of realizing these. She *is* funny, however. Like William, she is sometimes an innocent abroad; but, unlike him, she concocts schemes that *always* work. She is treated too kindly by her author, and the stories about her lack the pile-up of farcical misunderstanding and events going wildly askew that makes the William stories so memorable.

In *Enter – Patricia*, the heroine is older than Felicity, but still representative of an attempt by Richmal to create an attractive girl series character. The wit of the stories wilts as the ineptitude of Patricia and 'darling' (her unnamed husband) grows. Both of them muddle dates and times; she is hopeless at dressmaking and most other domestic chores; he is so unmechanical that when a watch goes wrong he doesn't even realize that it simply needs winding. All this would have worked quite well if Patricia had been William's age instead of a full-grown woman. Like Veronica and Felicity, Patricia starred only in sufficient episodes to fill one book; perhaps if Richmal hadn't been quite so busy with William and her serious family sagas she would have hammered these heroines into better shape in future stories. As it is we can only catch glimpses in the William books (with Violet Elizabeth and – briefly – William's cousin Dorita) of Richmal's capacity to create a strong-minded and believable girl character who would be worthy of a leading role.

Richmal was at first made form mistress of the lower third, but she taught classics, her special subject, to the older girls. She also gave English lessons to some of them. Joan Braunholtz recollects how much she loved these classes with Richmal, particularly when they were studying Tennyson's *Idylls of the King*. This favourite book of Richmal's crops up both seriously and as a stimulation for comical events in several of her books, from *Anne Morrison* to the William stories:

> 'A Knight,' said Miss Drew, who was struggling to inspire her class with enthusiasm for Tennyson's *Idylls of the King*, 'a Knight was a person who spent his time going round succouring the oppressed.'
>
> 'Suckin' wot?' said William, bewildered.
>
> 'Succour means help. He spent his time helping anyone who was in trouble.'
>
> 'How much did he get for it?' asked William.

However, despite the banality that William injects into the medieval mythology so beloved by Miss Drew (and Richmal), his latent chivalrous impulses *are* stirred by tales of knightly courage and then, of course, he can't wait to emulate them. The hilarious results of his excursions into Arthurian adventure are entertainingly chronicled both in 'The Knight at Arms' (from *More William*) and 'The Knights of the Square Table' (from *William the Bad*).

The Grail mythology was used more seriously by Richmal as a symbol of idealism in the context of wartime sacrifice. It seems on the surface as if the Great War did not touch the Lamburn family too deeply; Jack, as mentioned before, had to stay in Rhodesia and was thus spared the hazards and horrors of trench warfare in France or Flanders; Gwen's husband, Thomas, was not conscripted, and there was no young man at the front to whom Richmal was romantically attracted. However, two of her cousins were killed, and, like everyone else in Britain, Richmal would have been only too painfully aware of the regular and dispiritingly lengthy casualty lists, and of the anguish that these represented to so many families. She touched on the subject of the war in some of her family sagas and – fleetingly and retrospectively – in one or two William episodes. In *Anne Morrison*, Sandy – too old to have joined up – possibly speaks about the war with Richmal's own voice, which is the somewhat reticent one of the spectator from the sidelines:

> It's not for me to talk about the war. I've been able to take no part in [it] . . . I don't deny that the ills of war outweigh the good . . . I only say there *is* good . . . we saw it even in this nightmare . . . right at the beginning, don't you remember? We got our values right – just for a minute. Just for a minute we saw materialism and idealism in their true colours . . . we all felt that we could die for our ideals – we were crusaders, we were the Knights of the Holy Grail . . . .

High flown, perhaps, but it is noteworthy that in the Second World War, when Winston Churchill tried to find words that would adequately describe the 'Few' – the fighter pilots of the Battle of Britain – he referred to them as modern day Knights of the Round Table.

More surprisingly, in *Anne Morrison*, Sandy talks of war as being 'a clean, healthy thing . . . War and Love are the two great realities of the Primitive man . . . You'll never eliminate war any more than you'll eliminate Love . . .'. He sees the 'good in war' as 'the splendour of idealism and self-sacrifice and comradeship and courage, that nothing else calls forth' as fully as war does.

In *The Wildings*, there is another reference to the heightened intensities of people's feelings during the 1914–18 war, which seems to have been inspired directly from an incident in Richmal's own life. Hero and Mr Moston are discussing the beauties of Paris, a city that they both know well:

> 'I was awfully struck by the devotion of the men and boys in the Paris Churches,' said Hero.
>
> 'Our training of the young in English public schools represses it,' said Mr. Moston. 'It's there – an enormous fount of it untapped. Look how it blazed out at the call of the

War. It was religious fervour as much as patriotic fervour. Of course, their services...'

'That's how God ought to be worshipped,' said Hero quickly, 'with colour and music and light.'

Richmal had spent a holiday in Paris in 1924 at a time in her life when she was facing the tremendous challenge of recent disablement (see page 109). That she was bowled over by the beauty of the Roman Catholic mass which she attended at the splendiferous church of Sacré-Coeur is clear from her account of it in her travel journal:

Boys and young men in church in Paris. There must be a touch of devotion and piety in boys and young men in England untapped and wasted. All the natural chivalry and devotion repressed by training. It blazed forth at the call of the war. To many it was a religious war needing a religious fervour. As the rich idle young flocked to the Crusades in the old days to sacrifice ease and luxury and comfort and life – so would the young do now if modern life made any calls on it, if that wonderful goal of devotion and self-sacrifice and idealism of youth were not allowed to die unused. Religion is too much repressed. Our clergy are too fond of trying to pose as men of the world.

And, referring to the Roman Catholic Service:

That is how God should be worshipped – with light and colour and music.

The wonderful beauty and intimacy of the exquisite little shrines with their blaze of candles like so many stars of hope and their ... band of apt and silent worshippers – the utter abandon and lack of self-consciousness of the worshipping – unmoved, unconsious of the ... staring and curious tourists who pass by.

Of course, she draws on this for the discussion in *The Wildings* betwen Hero and Mr Motson. In the Sacré-Coeur experience, one sees glimpses of Richmal's religious passion, which is normally quietly contained within her Anglicanism. It is interesting to compare her response to the 'boys and young men in church in Paris' with her descriptions of another boy (William) at his Sunday morning devotions. She tells us that William in church enjoys singing psalms and hymns, and that any stone-deaf person could have told when William was singing 'by the expressions of pain on the faces of those around him'. Apparently his voice is not only discordant but loud enough to drown the organ *and* the choir. He considers listening to the sermon a waste of time, so during this he either stares at the curate (who goes pink with embarrassment under the onslaught of William's gaze) or holds face-pulling competitions with one of the choirboys. Sometimes he amuses himself with the insects he brings into church with him in a matchbox in his pocket. In one hilarious episode, William carries his white rat, Rufus, in his pocket, and surreptitiously tries to teach it to dance in his pew. The congregation is electrified by the sight of Rufus wriggling out of William's grasp, leaping onto Mr Brown's balding pate (to an accompaniment of Ethel's screams), running along the rim of the pulpit, and then being snaffled by one of William's traditional choirboy enemies.

All this seems a far cry from the subjects that Richmal listed in her Bromley High School teaching notebook for the intellectual stimulation of her students – 'Discuss the influence of the geographical position of Rome on its political history', etc. Her period at the High School was a happy and fulfilling one. She loved her work, and was, according to her colleagues and her pupils, a gifted teacher. Also, because she was now in a day-school, she could spend more time with her family than when she had been working at St Elphin's. She and Clara lived harmoniously together at Cherry Orchard Road, and Gwen and little Tommy were not far away.

Richmal's popularity (as Miss Lamburn) at the High School is evident from jottings in the school magazine. She took an active part in many aspects of school life, teaching hockey as well as playing it, helping for several years to organize the debating society, and lending a hand at sales of work organized by the school in aid of charity: 'Miss Drake and Miss Lamburn presided over a stall for household utensils ... Practically

61

everything was sold, and the sum of £152. 1s. 11d. realized.'
(This type of activity must have been very useful as background
for William's frequent participation in village bazaars and sales
of work.) Her love of classical drama led her to take parties of
girls to see performances of *Medea*, *Alcestis*, etc., at a time when
the school did not organize very many outings, and she also
became involved at a practical level in theatricals. A July 1922
issue of the magazine states:

> The Dramatic Society gave two performances of 'A
> Midsummer Night's Dream' at the end of the summer term
> 1921. The society was then on trial, as it was its first under-
> taking. However, thanks to the timely aid of Miss Lamburn
> during the last week of rehearsals, and the keenness of all
> concerned – actors, understudies and scene-shifters alike – it
> was a great success and a considerable sum was raised, which
> was devoted to school needs . . . Miss Lamburn has now very
> kindly become a permanent member of the Committee, and is
> a most indefatigable 'coach' and stage-manager.

Richmal wrote about some of these activities a decade later, in
1933, on the occasion of the school's fiftieth anniversary.
Incidentally her memory seems slightly faulty regarding the first
play that the dramatic society presented, which was not *As You
Like It* but *A Midsummer Night's Dream*:

> The Dramatic Society was originally started by a group of the
> elder girls. They chose 'As You Like It', assigned the parts,
> rehearsed it, and had got it well under weigh before they
> called me in as producer shortly before the performance – in
> order, I believe, to have someone to blame in case by any
> unlikely chance the thing turned out a failure. It was far from
> being a failure, and they followed it by excellent performances
> of 'The Rivals', 'The Merchant of Venice', and scenes from
> 'Emma'. I don't remember any contretemps in connection
> with these except the accidental breaking of a plaster cast – I
> think it was the Venus de Milo – that we had borrowed from
> the studio without permission, to enhance the effect of a
> moonlit garden. I confessed this to Miss Richardson on the

Monday morning in a state of almost hysterical abjectness, and she was very nice about it.

I remember delightful meetings of – was it called the Literary Society? – at which we read large portions of Dickens and Jane Austen novels, some of us taking the characters and others reading the narrative. I still have glorious memories of Miss Hodge [the headmistress] as Sarah Gamp and Serjeant Buzfuz.

In the same recollective article, she also writes about the debating society, and how she primed members of her form during the lunch recess on debate days, and then 'fixed them with a stern eye till they had actually made these prepared contributions to the discussion. The most spirited debate I can remember was on the League of Nations, and I much regret to have to place on record that I both spoke and voted against that excellent institution.' The real high spots of this particular society, however, seem to have been less formal occasions, which she goes on to describe:

The Debating Society used to have a picnic in the summer when it would lie on Keston Common, gorged with sandwiches and cherries, and debate on subjects drawn at random out of an envelope. Five minutes – or was it ten? – were given to each subject. I remember a keen discussion on 'That the social side of school life is more important than the lessons', to which a party of stray picnickers listened in dumb but open-mouthed amazement.

Joan Braunholtz remembers Richmal's kindness to her when, at the age of eleven, she was unhappy and without friends at the High School. Somehow, as they walked home together after hockey at school, Richmal found things to say that made Joan feel 'encouraged and stimulated'. She opened the girls' eyes to the beauties not only of Latin and Greek but to those of their own language. When one of them, an agnostic, protested about having to sing hymns at prayers, Richmal urged: 'Never mind the hymns; the collects are wonderful English.' Greek, however, was her great love. 'She told us all in the Latin class how much more wonderful Greek was – and Greek with her was a most wonderful experience ... We read *Antigone* (Sophocles) and Homer.'

Sadly, however, Richmal's teaching career was unexpectedly curtailed after less than ten years in all. In the summer of 1923 she was unwell with what seemed to be a particularly virulent cold. Clara took her to a guest-house in Cromer to recuperate, but was horrified to find that, far from getting better, her daughter was becoming gravely ill. Somehow she got her back to Bromley, and nursed her at home. Only then did Clara discover that Richmal had been struck down by poliomyelitis (or infantile paralysis, as it was then commonly called). There was no immunization in the 1920s against this dreaded disease, which nearly always left the sufferer with some degree of disablement. Richmal lost the use of her right leg, which remained immobile for the rest of her life, so that she was always lame and had to walk with a stick.

For a young, active and attractive young woman like Richmal, the effects of polio added up to the double tragedy of disablement and the deformity of an awkward and permanently stiff leg. She faced her situation, however, with characteristic calmness and courage. As soon as she was strong enough she started to take taxis or to cycle (with her 'dead' leg sticking out at odd and perilous angles) the 3½-mile journey to school and back. She was particularly concerned about the three girls who had passed their Higher Schools Certificate and were halfway through the university scholarship year. As Audrey Carr wrote (in an obituary tribute to Richmal in the school magazine of 1968–9) she 'showed wonderful courage'; she would 'drag her paralysed leg on crutches to a classroom and take Latin with these three for three solid periods, teaching them more than Latin by her courage and cheerfulness. . . . It was indeed a privilege to know R.C.L., not only on account of her literary eminence but for her own delightful self.'

Another of Richmal's former pupils says that 'Miss Lamburn ... was by far the most lasting influence on my life. Her serene and happy temperament and deep faith in the essential rightness of things had a special value for girls at a difficult age. Her love of literature – English, Latin, but most of all Greek, was infectious, and Greek with her was one of the most precious experiences ...' She recalls with regret that Miss Lamburn's 'true vocation for teaching' had to be cut short by her illness.

The attack of polio did indeed mark a turning-point in Richmal's life. After some months of struggling to get to the High School and back on her bicycle, her doctor urged her to give up her teaching job, which he felt was putting her under far too much strain. And fortunately another satisfying career was available to her, though she did not know how lucrative it might turn out to be. William had already been well and truly launched (see page 68); Richmal had achieved a measure of success with her writing, and now she would be able to give all her energies to it.

Teaching's loss was literature's gain. Years later, when her niece and namesake Richmal Crompton Lamburn Disher (Gwen and Thomas's third child, later Richmal Ashbee) said 'what a shame it was' that she had become disabled, the indefatigable and irrepressible creator of William was able honestly to reply: 'But I have had a more interesting life because of it.'

As a postscript to Richmal's teaching career, the comments of her two headmistresses are worth noting. Miss Hodge (of Bromley High School) commenting on Richmal's intelligence said, 'I can't understand why Miss Lamburn's books aren't better'; and Miss Flood, after Richmal had been writing William stories for some time, merely said that this literary activity 'was like a Juggernaut's car'. (However, Lady Sybil Osmond very much doubts if Margaret Flood ever brought herself to read a William book.) In fact, even before Richmal underwent the ravages of polio, Miss Hodge had been suggesting that she should give up writing, which was taking up more and more of her time, to concentrate on teaching. Her editors, on the other hand, were urging her to stop being a school-marm and to give herself entirely to writing. It seems as if the final decision was taken out of her hands by personal disaster – and the strange dealings of destiny.

CHAPTER 5

WILLIAM: DREAM CHILD OR NIGHTMARE?

"You're only putting a little on, aren't you?"
Georgie asked anxiously.
"Oh, yes, Georgie," William reassured him—"only
a little."

At first, after leaving the High School (to take up 'Literary Work', as the school staff register put it), Richmal still gave a little coaching at her home to older students. This arrangement came to an end when Miss Hodge retired in 1924 and Miss Littlewood replaced her.

Richmal was already writing regular William stories for the *Happy Mag.*, a George Newnes publication, although this is not where William's saga began. She had had more than one go at creating an iconoclastic anti-hero. Fairly soon after her story 'Thomas' had seen the light of day in the *Girl's Own Paper*, another of her tales about a boy in revolt against adult authority appeared. This was 'One Crowded Hour', which was published in the September 1918 issue of *Woman at Home* in the name of R. C. Lamburn. It featured two children, who can quickly be seen as forerunners of William and Violet Elizabeth Bott. In 'One Crowded Hour', these characters are called Robert Green, and Marie Elizabeth:

> Marie Elizabeth was the good girl of the neighbourhood. She had short, bobbing, fluffy golden curls, big blue eyes – and a mouth like a cherub's. She wore short – very short, gossamer embroidered frocks which stood out stiffly like little ballet skirts, and showed a multitude of the daintiest soft frills. . . . She was never seen with a speck of dirt upon her spotless white attire . . . Marie Elizabeth herself was never rude, never rough, never dirty, and never greedy . . .

And, at the other end of the scale,

> Robert Green was the bad boy of the neighbourhood. He was always rude, always rough, always dirty, and always greedy. Mothers who wished for well-behaved children kept their offspring away from Robert Green as carefully as if he had measles or the whooping cough . . .

Robert, of course, is the raw and rather rough material from which Richmal would eventually perfect William. And Marie Elizabeth turns out to resemble the later and more sophisticated 'sweet little girl in white' not only in sartorial matters. Like Violet Elizabeth, she lisps; like her too, despite her frilly and frothy appearance, she has a tough streak and cannot easily be repressed, as her encounter with the rowdy Robert demonstrates:

> 'Do you like me?' she inquired.
> 'No,' he shouted. '*Hate* you – you *ugly* ole thing.'
> 'Don't mind,' said Marie Elizabeth sweetly. 'Leth play gameth, thall we?'

And they do – to the detriment of her gossamer garb and

golden curls. These, after exposure to the exploits organized by Robert – bear-hunting, playing Red Indians, mucking about in muddy streams, picking wild brambles and the like – are damaged beyond recognition. But both the fluffy little female and the scruffy small boy have enjoyed their escapade.

This was Robert Green's only published adventure, but the more resilient character that he heralded appeared in print soon afterwards in a story called 'Rice-Mould' in the February 1919 edition of the Newnes *Home Magazine*. There was then no going back. William Brown, his family, friends and enemies, and his village's bizarre assortment of earnest aesthetes, peppery ex-military gentlemen, nervous clerics, intense spinsters, batty artists and bright young things, quickly caught the imagination of a large and loyal readership. The *Home Magazine* catered for adults, and Richmal's William stories in it were for mature readers rather than for children. The stories were transferred to the *Happy Mag.* in 1922, where they ran until the magazine ended in the wartime paper shortages of 1940. The *Happy Mag.* was the kind of periodical that appealed to the whole family. Despite Richmal's satiric style and demanding vocabulary, children, as well as their parents, began to turn with relish to the pages that provided the regular William story. The Newnes editorial staff got the message; in May 1922 twelve of the already published stories were collected (in somewhat arbitrary order) in a half-crown hardback entitled *Just – William*, and in the following month fourteen further stories appeared in *More William*. Both books were designed to appeal to the juvenile market, and new titles were published at regular intervals for the rest of Richmal's life. *William the Lawless*, the thirty-eighth and last of these collections of short stories, was published posthumously in 1970. (In fact, number 26 in the series, *Just William's Luck, 1948* is not a selection of short stories, but a full-length novel; one or two of its chapters are based on a previously published complete episode, however. There is also an extra William book, which is not generally counted as part of the series. This is *Just William – The Story of the Film*, 1939.)

From 1919 until well into the 1940s the stories retained the wit and verve that had delighted adult readers of the *Home Magazine* and *Happy Mag.* Afterwards, when Richmal was writing the tales for direct publication in children's books, their content and construction became less intricate, and, although still highly entertaining, the stories moved a step away from satire towards slapstick. But there was no lessening of the popularity of the books after the *Happy Mag.* folded. Sales remained high until the saga finished, and early stories continued to be reprinted. Between 1919 – when William first bounced belligerently onto the literary scene – and the early 1980s, over nine million copies of the books, including translated editions, had been distributed. Since 1983 when Macmillan began reprinting titles in both hard-covers and paper-backs a further half million copies have been sold.

Richmal's first novel for adults, *The Innermost Room*, appeared in bookshops in the year following *Just – William*. From then until the end of the 1960s, she was always working on two books at the same time – one (generally about William) for children, and the other for adult readers. For the latter she produced 41 novels and 9 short-story collections (see appendix, on pages 162–4). It was always her hope to produce memorable fiction for adults, and she remarked on more than one occasion that she regarded William as a 'pot-boiler'. Ironically, of course, it is the William stories that survive and flourish, while her more serious novels are rarely reprinted. These deal interestingly enough with the mores of pre-1939 middle-class English life, but the mood is generally one of acceptance rather than enquiry, so that the books have a certain inbuilt obsolescence. Conversely, the William stories, which were designed as ephemeral reading matter, transcend the social restraints of their period and setting. Incisive observation and facetious comment are combined with startling effectiveness. Seen with hindsight, the William episodes are virtual parodies of Richmal's adult family sagas – drawing-room dramas transmogrified into rugged comedy, with William as the ingenuous initiator of social chaos and embarrassment for his elders. The genteel environment of the cook-gardener-and-housemaid-employing class makes William's rebellious non-conformity far more effective than if he came from a working-class family. In the early 1920s, William was something new in children's fiction, and a welcome relief from the impeccably honourable (or sentimentalized) boys and girls who had for so long been the leading characters in juvenile books. William's gut honesty and gritty practicality were bound to be appreciated:

> 'Do you mean to tell me you want to be paid for doing a simple thing like that?'
> 'Yes,' replied William simply.

Richmal might have started off by seeing William as a potboiler but the stories never seemed formula-ridden or lacking in zest and originality. There were times when Richmal implied that, far from being someone she was fond of, William was in fact her 'Frankenstein monster', whom she'd tried unsuccessfully to banish from her life. On other occasions, however, she speaks of him (and boyhood in general) with enormous understanding and affection. On balance, he seems to slot more firmly into the category of dream child than nightmare. Without at first realizing it, Richmal managed to make her pot-boiler into an archetype of the unbookish, adventurous outdoor boy, whose appeal was to cross wide social and generational gaps. Above all, of course, William and his enterprises are wonderfully funny and inventive. From the beginning, Richmal displayed a Wodehouse-like flair for facetious description of the farcical pile-up of odd events that William so often initiates.

William has his own very vivid personality, quite distinct from that of any other fictional, or real, character, even though so many of his exploits were inspired by Richmal's brother. He carries dirtiness and dishevelment to the point of fetishism; he is aggressive, opinionated and obstructionist. However, he can also be helpful and well-meaning, even though his attempts to be useful generally misfire:

> 'I've took a lot of trouble trying to get [Ethel] married,' said William, 'and this is how she pays me! . . . She's turning out an old maid an' it's not my fault . . . Seems to me she's goin' to go on livin' in our house all her life till she dies, an' that's a nice look out for me, isn't it?'

A strong, if cockeyed, sense of fair play motivates William, and often causes him to resent the hidebound adults who restrict his creative pursuits by confiscating his bugles, catapults, insect collections, pen-knives and pop-guns.

Early in William's history, Richmal made an attempt to bring his saga to an end. After only five episodes she told her editor that she'd had enough of William; he, however, suggested that even if William no longer starred in her stories he should at least be brought into them in a minor role. But, as Richmal explained many years later, 'of course, William could do nothing else but dominate the whole thing once he'd been let in'. In the 1920s and 1930s, she still hoped some day to produce profound novels; her personal tastes in reading remained serious and scholarly, but her determined, indomitable and occasionally disaster-prone dream child dug himself well into her life, and, in her own words, 'like all characters who have been over-indulged by their authors, he insisted on having his own way'.

Her initial reluctance to maintain the fictional boy whom she had conceived makes it clear that he was in no way a substitute for any real-life son she might have liked to have. Her affection for, and interest in, children was largely fulfilled through her relationship with the Disher offspring (Tommy now had two sisters, Margaret and Richmal) to whom she appears from the beginning to have been an ideal aunt. Thomas Disher's wide range of business interests took him frequently away from home, and his absences helped to sustain the closeness which had always existed between Richmal and her sister. Men and marriage did not seem to figure in Richmal's scheme of things. As long as she was working in the residential set-up at St Elphin's, her opportunities of meeting men had been extremely restricted, and even when she was teaching at Bromley on a day-school basis her social contacts were limited. She was busy with after-hours activities at the High School, and with her writing; also, Clara didn't like to be left on her own for long periods, and Richmal respected this.

Now well into her thirties, she was becoming a highly successful writer of popular fiction, contributing stories to various magazines on a regular basis, and having her novels well received. She relished her financial independence, and only three years after retiring from teaching was able to have The

Glebe, a large and gracious house standing in its own grounds, built for herself and Clara in Oakley Road, Bromley Common. The Dishers had also moved from Denmark Hill to Bromley, nearer to Richmal and her mother.

Richmal's fears that Thomas was not the right husband for Gwen began to seem justified. He spent more and more time away from home, and Richmal suspected that other women as well as business interests were keeping him from his family. (It has been suggested that Richmal's dislike of the hearty and overconfident Thomas, who seems to have stimulated some of the less sympathetic male characters in her novels, might have influenced her in opting for the unmarried state. This, however, hardly seems likely as she seemed to like men as companions, and to be very much at ease with them.) Motivated by her customary generosity and a desire to give Gwen and her children as much security as possible, in 1932 Richmal bought a house for them in Cumberland Road, Bromley. It was to remain the Disher family home until the early 1980s, but Thomas senior was not there for long. He and Gwen were divorced in 1935, a break-up which she accepted without bitterness, and about which he was to comment, with characteristic complacency, in his 1954 autobiography: '. . . had I been a schoolmaster or bank official or had any other occupation with more or less regular working hours, had I not such a strong antipathy to tobacco and alcohol, my first marriage might not have ended.' But end it did; the gap left by Thomas's departure seems to have closed quickly, and Richmal became even more involved with the fortunes of Gwen and the children. Much as she loved her literary work, she always maintained that people were more important, and she gave freely of her time and energies to her family. In return she drew tremendous emotional satisfaction from them.

Meanwhile, her fictional dream child went from strength to strength. Richmal's insights into childhood were expressed through juvenile characters in many of her adult novels and short stories, but nowhere more persuasively than in the William books. She was occasionally asked by the media to comment upon her most celebrated characterization, and the following extracts from an article entitled 'Meet William' (published in the

Collectors' Digest Annual for 1962) indicate the depth of feeling that she had for William:

> He has been called 'the bad boy of fiction' but he is not so black as he is painted. His insatiable curiosity may put the refrigerator out of action, immobilize the Hoover and fuse the electric lights, but it is the spirit of the inventor and pioneer that inspires his work of destruction. He explores unknown stretches of country, plunging into ditches, climbing trees, doing battle with his enemies, and comes home a sight to break his mother's heart, but his courage and initiative are the stuff of which heroes are made. He has sudden impulses to 'help' his family. He 'helps' to wash up and leaves a trail of broken crockery in his wake; he 'helps' to bring in the coal, covering face, hands and the kitchen floor; he 'helps' bring in the deck chairs, becoming inextricably entangled with each; he puts in a spot of gardening and no one can ever use the secateurs again. It is not always easy to remember how laudable his intentions were. . . .
>
> There is a theory that, on our way from the cradle to the grave, we pass through all the stages of evolution, and the boy of eleven is at the stage of the savage – loyal to his tribe, ruthless to his foes, governed by mysterious taboos, an enemy of civilization and all its meaningless conventions.

William has made this same point in his own inimitable vocabulary: 'I don't WANT to behave like a civilized yuman bein'. I'd rather be a savage any day. I bet savages don't let themselves be dragged off to dotty ole women when they'd rather go to see blood-curdlin' an' nerve-shattcrin' Westerns.'
Richmal continues:

> He dislikes little girls, not only because he considers them to belong to an inferior order of being but also because he suspects them of being allies of the civilization that threatens his liberty.

This fearful and feminine threat to William's freedom is em-bodied in a variety of village stereotypes, such as Miss Milton, the vinegary and boy-hating spinster, and Mrs Monks, the vicar's wife who, after having various Sunday school and other church functions wrecked by the Outlaws, feels justified in foiling their knavish tricks. And lots of those ladies who are taken up with Higher Thought or Perfect Love or Psychic Phenomena ('I firmly believe that Colonel Henks's spirit is trying to attract my attention') have strong cause for wanting to curtail William's liberty. The direst threat to his noble- (or ignoble-) savage state, however, comes in the frill-bedecked and diminutive bundle of precocity that is Violet Elizabeth Bott, the only daughter of the *nouveau riche* sauce magnate who with his family comes to take up residence at the Hall. William and Violet Elizabeth's first meeting is a classic example of the clash between the sexes. Forced by his mother to accompany her to tea with Mrs Bott and her small daughter, William finds his worst fears about girlish ghastliness realized in Violet Elizabeth. She has bubbly fair curls which glow like a golden halo, a pink and white face that shines with cleanliness, and a filmy white lace-trimmed dress, from the ballet-type skirts of which peep silk-socked legs and white buckskin shoes. William's horror at her appearance intensifies when she asks his name and he learns that she lisps. Violet Elizabeth, unabashed by his terse replies, continues the conversation:

'How old are you?'
'Eleven.'
'My nameth Violet Elizabeth.'
He received the information in silence.
'I'm thix.'
He made no comment. He examined the distant view with an abstracted frown.
'Now you muth play with me.'
William allowed his cold glance to rest upon her.
'I don't play little girls' games,' he said scathingly. But Violet Elizabeth did not appear to be scathed.
'Don' you know any little girlth?' she said pityingly. 'I'll teach you little girlth gameth,' she added pleasantly.
'I don't *want* to,' said William. 'I don't *like* them. I don't *like* little girls' games. I don't want to know 'em.'

74

Violet Elizabeth gazed at him open-mouthed.

'Don't you *like* little girlth?' she said.

'*Me?*' said William with superior dignity. 'Me? I don't know anything about 'em. Don't want to.'

'D—don't you like me?' quavered Violet Elizabeth in incredulous amazement. William looked at her. Her blue eyes filled slowly with tears, her lips quivered.

'I like you,' she said, 'Don't you like me?'

William stared at her in horror.

'You—you *do* like me, don't you?'

William was silent.

A large shining tear welled over and trickled down the small pink cheek.

'You're making me cry,' sobbed Violet Elizabeth. 'You are. You're making me cry, 'cause you won't thay you like me.'

'I—I do like you,' said William desperately. 'Honest — I do. Don't cry. I do like you. Honest!'

A smile broke through the tear-stained face.

'I'm tho glad,' she said simply. 'You like all little girlth, don't you?' She smiled at him hopefully. 'You do, don't you?'

William, pirate and Red Indian and desperado, William, woman-hater and girl-despiser, looked round wildly for escape and found none. Violet Elizabeth's eyes filled with tears again.

'You *do* like all little girlth, don't you? she persisted with quavering lip. 'You do, don't you?'

It was a nightmare to William. They were standing in full view of the drawing-room window. At any moment a grown-up might appear. He would be accused of brutality, of making little Violet Elizabeth cry. And, strangely enough, the sight of Violet Elizabeth with tear-filled eyes and trembling lips made him feel that he must have been brutal indeed. Beneath his horror he felt bewildered.

'Yes, I do,' he said hastily 'I do. Honest I do.'

She smiled again radiantly through her tears. 'You with you wath a little girl, don't you?'

'Er—yes. Honest I do,' said the unhappy William.

'Kith me,' she said raising her glowing face.

William was broken.

He brushed her cheek with his.

This, of course, is Violet Elizabeth in fairly gentle mood. More generally her way of blackmailing William and the Outlaws is her celebrated threat 'to thcream, an' thcream' till she's sick, if she can't get her way. She is a cross that William frequently has to bear. He never likes her, but he can never entirely escape her clutches. She and the 'civilizing influence' that she quirkily represents hang over him rather like Nemesis.

If there has to be any female influence in his life, he is much happier with the unshowy, meekly adoring, dark-haired little girl next door, Joan Clive (or Crewe or Parfitt – see page 84). She is the only female member of the Outlaws, not quite a fully fledged one, but useful, for example, in assuming the supportive role of squaw when the boys are playing Red Indians:

> To Joan, William was a god-like hero. His very wickedness partook of the divine . . . She looked at him silently, hoping that he would deign to tell her his thoughts, but not daring to ask. Joan held no modern views on the subject of equality of the sexes.

In some episodes, William, through Joan's eyes, is seen as a 'lord of creation'.

William, Ginger, Henry and Douglas all appreciate her tractability and passivity. With the exception of Joan, his mother and – briefly – the various females with whom he becomes infatuated, William has few good things to say of the fair sex: 'They're soppy an' batty and stuck up an' stupid . . . They can't play fair or talk sense.' He is particularly contemptuous of women who imagine themselves to be beautiful, like his sister Ethel, whom he imitates to her chagrin by rolling up his eyes and assuming 'the expression commonly attributed to a dying duck in a thunderstorm'. When William *does* go to enormous lengths to get some girl or another out of a scrape, his efforts – even when successful – often stimulate the scornful fury of the object of his attentions rather than the gratitude that he might justifiably expect.

But, despite such stereotyping, from the beginning the William books have been popular with girls as well as boys. They do not appear to resent the proliferation of huffy, contrary-minded female scatterbrains and social climbers, vamps and vampires who flutter and flatter and batter their way through the saga. It must be said, of course, that Richmal makes exuberantly effective use of these feminine stereotypes (and of masculine ones too).

Although she taught girls for nearly ten years, and obviously had a great understanding of them, Richmal never managed to produce a girl character who came anywhere near to being as engaging and addictive as William. Later in the 1920s she made two or three attempts at creating lively young heroines (see page 56) but it was boyhood that claimed her real sympathy and interest. It is an intriguing thought that one of the most appealing little girls in literature, Carroll's Alice, was dreamed up by a man, while William, who is certainly one of the most popular of all fictional boys, was created by a woman. It is tempting to see these literary creations as anima – or animus – projections on the part of their authors; in Richmal's case, however, we can be fairly sure that William is *not* a representation of her ideals of masculinity. He can so often be seen as the distinct antithesis of herself – the direct opposite that clashes rather than complements. He is intellectually lazy while she is studious; socially obstructive while she is co-operative; unbookish to the point of philistinism while she is extremely literary and cultured – and so on. The lists of contrasts between them is endless.

In Richmal's already quoted article for the *Collectors' Digest Annual*, she goes on to say of the human boy in general and of William by implication that:

> . .beneath his tough exterior, he is sensitive, generous and affectionate, though he has, too, a pride that makes him conceal these qualities. You can hurt him desperately by a careless word, but you will never know that you have done so. Moreover, despite his outrageous appearance and behaviour, he has a strong sense of dignity that you affront at your peril.

All this hardly suggests resentment on her part of William as a pot-boiler, or as some sort of monster who took over her life and prevented her from writing great novels.

She has the gift of encapsulating the essence of boyhood in a very few words:

'What'll we do this morning,' said Ginger. It was sunny. It was holiday time. They had each other and a dog. Boyhood could not wish for more. The whole world lay before them.

And, a little later on in the same book, Richmal describes William and the Outlaws 'scuffling, shuffling, dragging their toes along the ground, whistling, pushing each other at intervals' as 'in the fashion of boyhood they made their way'.

She also, of course, frequently conveys the activities of the Outlaws in facetious terms: 'In their shrinking from the glare of publicity they showed an example of unaffected modesty that many other public societies might profitably emulate.' This reticence is simply because William, Ginger, Henry and Douglas know that keeping a low profile is the best, in fact the only, way of keeping their parents out of their affairs. Richmal was one of the first authors to make good use in her stories of the childhood group or gang. As early as 1908, when he drew up his basic principles for scouting, General Sir Robert (later Lord) Baden-Powell stressed the importance for boys of such group activities.* Forerunners of the gang in early children's fiction were simply groups of brothers (and sometimes sisters) from the same family, who were united in some escapade or other. School story writers also took up the theme, with a variety of famous 'Co.s', and, also before William's advent, comic papers provided gangs from the rumbustious late-Victorian 'Ball's Pond Banditti' in *Larks* to the cosily anthropomorphic 'Tiger Tim & Co.' in the *Rainbow*. Few writers, however, have conveyed the genuine atmosphere of the small boys' gang as accurately as Richmal.

Shoving and jostling each other, both figuratively and physically, the Outlaws never overtly express their mutual affection or solidarity. But they always remain a closely bound group. William, resilient, imaginative and optimistic, is always the leader (though when occasionally a string of his schemes

---

* Early in the saga, William is shown as a boy scout who likes constantly to be seen in his uniform. This is somewhat surprising, for William rarely shows signs of the self-discipline that serious scouting demands. Richmal, however, quickly debunks his scouting prowess: twigs for his fires won't ignite; handkerchiefs – made decrepit by William's customary depredations – don't work too well for tying knots; and so on.

1   Richmal Crompton in 1929.

2 (top) The Victorian family at Bury, Lancashire. Richmal Crompton herself is the little girl with a fringe sitting on the grass in the foreground. Her mother Clara and father Edward are on the extreme left, and her grandmother, the first Richmal Crompton, is seated at the centre.

3 (bottom left) Richmal's sister Gwen and brother Jack.

4 (bottom right) Richmal's family, early 1900s. She is sitting at the right of the picture, together with her father, mother, brother and sister.

(top) Richmal *circa* 1896, on the right, together with her brother Jack, the first model for William, and her sister Gwen.

(bottom left) Tom Disher, Richmal's nephew and Gwen's son, some time in 1928. He was the second model for William.

7 (bottom right) Richmal as a student in 1912.

8   (top) 'Stand up for St Elphin's.' Richmal is a young student teacher in this 1911 photogra
taken at St Elphin's, Darley Dale, Derbyshire. She is seated in the second row from the front, ni
from the left.

9   (bottom) St Elphin's School reunion, London, 1950. Richmal stands at third from left in
front row, next to Margaret Flood, the headmistress who banned Richmal's books because she
she had been parodied in *Anne Morrison*.

10 (top) Bromley High School for Girls, where Richmal taught from 1917 to 1924.

11 (bottom) Richmal as a form mistress at Bromley High, 1921.

12 (top left) Two Richmals with a crocodile, early 1930s. Richmal Crompton with her niece, Richmal Disher, daughter of Gwen.

13 (top right) With Ming in the garden of The Glebe, mid-1940s.

14 (bottom) The back garden of The Glebe, Bromley, Kent, with Richmal sitting at the centre of the picture. The remarkable success of her William books is evidenced by the fact that she was able to have this house built for her in its own acre of ground as early as 1927.

(top) Richmal and Edward Ashbee, her great-nephew and the third inspiration for William, outside her home at Beechworth, Chislehurst.

16   (bottom) The successful author meets some of her fans.

ENTER—
PATRICIA

2/6

RICHMAL
CROMPTON

ENTER—
PATRICIA
By
RICHMAL
CROMPTON

NEWNES

17. Dust jacket for *Enter-Patricia* (1927), one of Richmal Crompton's novels for adults. William

misfire he has to pull out all the stops to prove that he is still worthy to hold his position at the top of the heap). Ginger is the faithful lieutenant, Henry the know-all, and Douglas the pessimist. Although their exploits occur in a rustic setting, they could be a group of boys from any city or suburb, from any public park or school playground.

Richmal saw gangs as one facet of quintessential boyhood, and dogs as another. Jumble, a not-too-bright but, in William's eyes, always beautiful mongrel, wags his way into the stories in a very disorderly manner. He is featured in *Just – William* (rabbiting in the woods with the Outlaws and rather ineptly chasing a butterfly and a bee, scratching up a molehill, and getting stung by a wasp), and then, some chapters later, he makes what is obviously supposed to be his debut. (This unfortunate tampering with the time-scale of William's adventures took place because of editorial carelessness when the *Home* and *Happy Mag.* stories were collected into books: it must have been extremely puzzling to child readers who would presume that the book format was the original one. There are further irritating anomalies in the story sequences of some other William books.)

William is in a dejected, rejected, misunderstood mood (Mr Brown has just confiscated his bows and arrows) when he meets Jumble. What small boy could resist such a dog?

> Something was coming down the road. It came jauntily with a light, dancing step, fox-terrier ears cocked, retriever nose raised, collie tail wagging, slightly dachshund body a-quiver with the joy of life.

When Jumble gives him an inviting bark of welcome, William's drooping spirits begin to lift. He 'had sometimes practised privately in readiness for the blissful day when Fate should present him with a real live dog of his own. So far Fate, in the persons of his father and mother, had been proof against all his pleading.' We are told that Jumble is one of the very few beings who fully appreciate William. And certainly William totally appreciates Jumble.

Of course, there are aspects of boyhood which William and

the Outlaws emphatically do *not* embody. Horribly precious and picturesque little boys, sporting velvet knickerbockers or satin suits, with golden ringlets or Dutch Boy coiffures, crop up frequently to put the Outlaws on their mettle. In *More William*, the exemplary Joan is visited by her cousin, Cuthbert; we know at once that he's unsympathetic because, although he is William's age, he has a gleaming halo of Mary Pickford curls and wears an embroidered tunic and white socks. He doesn't enjoy playing 'rough gameth' – 'Let's thit down an' I'll tell you fairy thorieth' – and William, who is at first jealous because Joan *seems* to like Cuthbert, soon makes the proverbial mincemeat of him. Joan is suitably congratulatory: '. . . he's going tomorrow, and I am glad. Isn't he a softie? Oh, William, I do *love* you, you do such '*citing* things!'

Later, when the Outlaws' parents are ruefully reflecting upon their offspring's many faults, they agree that 'the Perfect Boy' does not exist. But then a smarmy little specimen called Georgie Murdoch (who never gets a speck of dirt on his aggressively white satin suits) comes to live at The Laurels with his besotted mother. He *is* the Perfect Boy. He becomes the idol of all the ladies of the village, and the Outlaws, fed up to the teeth with maternal urgings that they should emulate this paragon, put William's leadership on the line. Either he finds a way to put down Georgie 'who gets sickniner an' sickniner', or he is no longer fit to be head of the Outlaws. Of course William salvages his honour. Georgie is determined to be voted the best actor in scenes from British history that the children are asked to present at a select garden party. William inveigles him into playing King John (*after* he 'loses his things in the Wash'), daubs him lavishly with mud and makes him say (in the William-induced belief that these are the names of his two courtiers) 'Oh, Dam and Blarst' before a large audience of shocked and shattered ladies. Georgie, fortunately, can never retrieve his lost reputation; even his perfect manners and charming smile could never wipe out 'the memory of that mud-caked little horror uttering horrible oaths before the assembled aristocrats of the village'. Georgie *has* to go. And his parents, after selling their house and taking off, tell their new neighbours that there hadn't been a boy in William's village 'fit for Georgie to associate with'.

The ultimate in Perfect (or perfectly awful) Boys comes in the shape of Richmal's parody of A. A. Milne's Christopher Robin, who appeared on the literary scene soon after her own anti-hero was established. In the course of the saga, she has several side-swipes at Milne's besmocked and whimsical embodiment of childish charm. (However, according to Joan Braunholtz, she is supposed to have loved *Now We Are Six*, because one of the poems in it had a metre taken from Horace.) She goes to town in *William the Pirate* with a very winsome (but inwardly downright nasty) small boy called Anthony Martin, who brags to the Outlaws that his mother writes 'literary stories and poems' about him that 'really cultured people buy'. To link Anthony Martin even more closely with Christopher Robin (and particularly when the latter is prayerfully engaged), there are descriptions of these 'literary' poems which are constructed around repeated lines like 'Anthony Martin is milking a cow'.

Some recording equipment is delivered, which is supposed to be used to preserve for posterity (and commercial gain) Anthony's reading of one of his mother's poems about him, called 'Homework': ('Anthony Martin is doing his sums . . .'). Instead, William manipulates events so that Anthony's beastly bullying of his long-suffering nurse is recorded, and ready to be used by the Outlaws in a spot of blackmail. Sobbing and stamping, kicking, biting and scratching, the spoiled little darling has to comply with their demands – or else.

Anthony's pristine (and prissy) appearance is the antithesis of William's, whose hair is uncontrollable, whose cap is crushed, whose tie is askew and whose socks are constantly slipping down because he uses his garters for catapults. Richmal's lively word pictures of William were perfectly matched by the zestful drawings of the Nottingham illustrator, Thomas Henry (whose full name was Thomas Henry Fisher). He took over the pictures when William was switched from the *Home* to the *Happy Mag.*; earlier, the stories were illustrated with charm but little edge by the woman artist L. Hocknell. Thomas Henry, who illustrated many other stories and features in the *Happy Mag.* of the 1920s and 1930s, was to remain the regular William artist literally until his death in 1962, when he was in his eighties. (He died whilst he was working on a William picture.) The Crompton–Henry collaboration, always conducted by correspondence as they never met until 1954 (see page 136), was harmonious and productive. Thomas Henry projected with panache the whole range of William's facial expressions (from unctuousness to outrage; from gloom to glee; and so on) and extravagant gestures. The image of William that is indelibly stamped on the minds of several generations derives not only from Richmal's talents but also from those of Thomas Henry. His pictures are as quintessential to the William books as Sidney Paget's illustrations were to the Sherlock Holmes adventures, or Leonard Shields's visualization of Billy Bunter was to the Greyfriars stories.

Richmal made the setting for William and the Outlaws an archetypal – if extremely elastic – English village of the 1920s and 1930s. Despite her statement that the village was unplanned, created in patches and not as a whole, she based it loosely on a real village in a remote part of Lincolnshire, which she remembered from childhood, when the Lamburn family stayed there during one of Edward's temporary curacies. William's village is furnished with the appropriate props of its period – the manor house, village and church halls, sweetshops and cinema, workmen's cottages, dogs and ditches, and it is surrounded by a proper quota of irate farmers, muddy fields, crumbling barns, woods and cows. In spite of its between-the-wars flavour, the saga is somehow timeless; in spite of its extreme Englishness, it has a touch of universality. William quickly became the hero of children (and adults) from different strata of British society, and in countries whose social structures were vastly different from William's community. His adventures were translated into some sixteen or seventeen languages and widely circulated.

One of the inexplicable aspects of William's appeal, or rather of his non-appeal, is that he has never caught on in the United States. His Englishness seems to be no bar to readers in places as far removed from Bury or Bromley Common as Iceland and India; it therefore appears odd that Americans do not respond to William's adventures.* P. G. Wodehouse's utterly English

---

* Richmal once suggested that this is because American youth 'leaps straight from the cradle to the petting party', thus psychologically bypassing the William period of boyhood.

characterizations are so popular there, yet Richmal's in the same ironic and engaging tradition, are not. There are times too when William is regarded as having links — somewhat tenuous, perhaps — with classic embodiments of American boyhood. Brian Sibley in a BBC radio programme, 'William Revisited', transmitted in 1984, called William 'the nearest British equivalent to America's Tom Sawyer'; and in 1965 Dan O'Neill described him in the *Guardian* as 'a Home Counties Huckleberry Finn'. There is even a certain similarity between the early William and Penrod Schofield, a popular boy character created by the American author Booth Tarkington in 1913. (Richmal, however, had no memory of ever reading Tarkington's stories before producing William.)

Over the years Richmal tried discreetly to give William's exploits a more up-to-date flavour. Between the wars he skirmished with adherents of cults that flourished then (spiritualists, the Society of Ancient Souls, and so on); much later on he becomes involved with protest marchers and pop singers and interplanetary travel. William's domestic arrangements too are brought into line with the modern world. In the early 1920s, his parents employ a resident cook, a house-parlour-maid, and a gardener. By the late 1960s Mrs Brown's workaday lot is lightened only by the very part-time labours of a rather gloomy daily char. Similarly, the Browns' home (The Hollies) began as an extremely spacious residence, which boasted a morning-room, dining-room, drawing-room, study and library (as well as kitchen, scullery, bedrooms and bathroom). It also had outbuildings of sheds, stables, and a summer-house used occasionally by William as his headquarters, although the old barn was the more usual venue for the Outlaws. With the passage of the years, William's home shrinks into a modest but solid semi-detached house.

At the end of the 1950s, spurred on by readers' letters pointing out discrepancies and contradictions in her narratives, Richmal started to list, analyse and correct the thirty-three William books in the series which had by then appeared. One reader had pointed out, for example, that in one of the books a girl had brown eyes which, after two pages, became blue. He later wrote to remark that in another story the owner of a lost dog wears a green hat, which two pages on has changed to red. (This is not so anomalous as an occurrence in an Enid Blyton book, when a pet animal apparently undergoes a spontaneous sex-change.) The task of correlation which Richmal set herself was never completed. She soon realized that it would take precious writing time, and, as she commented earlier, she was generally quite happy not to have to consider her fictional settings in too much detail. She got as far as noting the fluctuation in Robert's age (17 or 18 or 19); that Ginger's surname arbitrarily altered from Flowerdew to Merridew, and back again; that stories mentioning Jumble came before his acquisition by William; that William sometimes attends a mixed and sometimes a single-sex school; that Joan – the little girl next door – is by turns surnamed Crewe, Clive or Parfitt; that Ethel is 19 (so are she and Robert twins?); and that Ronald Bell is occasionally a small boy but sometimes a grown-up colleague of Robert's. Richmal also started to list Robert's girlfriends (she got as far as twenty-four), Ethel's admirers (this time she gave up at twelve), and some of her girl chums. She listed Henry's relations (but not his small sister, who so frequently crops up), those of Violet Elizabeth and Ginger, and some of the 'places around William's home'.

Few of these discrepancies seriously frustrate readers, and Richmal decided not to pursue them throughout the whole of the saga. There are no inconsistencies, however, in her presentation of the natural language or jargon of childhood. She hit upon a stylized and simplistic method of conveying this; William's conversations and monologues do not strictly accord with street or playground speech, but they vividly put across the appropriate atmosphere. William makes many of his points by dogged repetition, which Richmal facetiously refers to as his 'dreaded eloquence'. In *Just – William*, the first of the books, William's style of rhetoric is subjected to narrative analysis: 'There was no doubt that when William condescended to adopt a phrase from any of his family's vocabularies, he considerably overworked it.' His inexorable flow of repetitive language in justification of one of his exploits is well illustrated in *Just –William* when he and his unusually robust girl cousin, Dorita, have deliberately ruined their bridal-attendant attire, in order to be spared the humiliation of appearing in public wearing 'soppy' white satin. William patiently and relentlessly explains what has happened, to his mother and the anguished, screeching bride-to-be, who is almost on her way to the church:

> 'We was walkin' round the room an' we sat down on the Chesterfield and there was this stuff on it an' it came on our clothes,' explained William stonily and monotonously and all in one breath.
>
> '*Why* did you sit down?' said his mother.
>
> 'We was walkin' round an' we jus' felt tired and we sat down on the Chesterfield and there was this stuff on it an' it came on –'
>
> 'Oh, *stop*! Didn't you *see* it there?' William considered.
>
> 'Well, we was jus' walking round the room,' he said, 'an' we jus' felt tired and we sat –'
>
> '*Stop* saying that.'

And, by the last book of all, William has lost none of his verbal energy. His grandiloquence in describing a characteristic accident – the upsetting by him of a workman's paint tin onto someone's head – takes up the best part of a page: 'I didn't know it was goin' to slip off and land on her head, did I? . . . There mus' have been somethin' wrong with the shape of it . . . It mus' have had a sort of bulge in the bottom to make it slip off like that an' land on her head. I'd hardly touched it' – and so on, and on, and on.

William has also been from the beginning the master of the misplaced statement, of misinterpretation, and of conscious (or unconscious) verbal obstructionism:

> '. . which of our grand national buildings have you seen?' said Mr Cranthorpe-Cranborough . . .
>
> 'I've never been to the races,' said William sadly,

He remains an embodiment of an extreme form of childhood logic. This, in combination with his capacity to get away with larger-than-life juvenile lawlessness, and his author's expertise in giving it all hilarious expression, guarantees the continuing appeal of Richmal's occasionally nightmarish dream child to boys, girls and grown-ups.

CHAPTER 6

HOME AND ABROAD

"You can look at the album while I am getting ready."
William was trapped, trapped in a huge and horrible
drawing-room, by a huge and horrible woman.

Life for Richmal and Clara at The Glebe settled into a pleasant and busy routine. Designed exactly for their needs, and standing in an acre of ground with an open and rural outlook, the house had few shortcomings. Of course, with her permanently straight and paralysed leg, Richmal couldn't tackle as many of the chores, especially those in the garden, as she would like to have done. She had to hire the services of a professional gardener two or three times a week (a happy arrangement, but doubtless one which evoked shades of William's running battles with the fictional and long-suffering gardener of the Brown family). In fact The Glebe in spaciousness and atmosphere was not unlike The Hollies – the house that William's family occupied at the beginning of the saga.

Clara managed most of the domestic indoor routine, while

Richmal enjoyed working outdoors, managing, despite her disability, to help practically as well as imaginatively in the planning and upkeep of the garden which was such a joy to her. Owning a place like The Glebe gave her enormous satisfaction. Few women in the 1920s and 1930s, let alone one who was handicapped, could by their own efforts and earnings have achieved Richmal's measure of financial independence and security.

Clara was firmly in charge of culinary affairs. Richmal used to speak self-deprecatingly of her own efforts to cook (although Richmal Ashbee says that her aunt was actually quite good in the kitchen). She claimed that she gave the results of one of her cooking sessions to the dog, who promptly buried it. Situations like this might have prompted her to bring William, occasionally, into the kitchen:

> William went over to the gas stove. There were two small saucepans, each containing dark brown stuff. They might as well be together, thought William, with a business-like frown. He poured the contents of one of the saucepans into the other. He had a moment's misgiving as the mingled smell of gravy and coffee arose from the mixture.

Richmal was no gourmet. One of the few things which she had in common with William was a taste for unexotic food, such as sweets and ice creams. She was particularly fond of the latter. Her family joked that she would consume ice cream with everything (and certainly, given half a chance, so would William). Richmal's long-standing favourite meal was roast beef, followed by strawberry jelly with ice cream; she was also fond of rump steak, with a dessert of chocolate éclairs. These two meals would seem equally fitting for William, but Richmal *did* draw the line at imbibing his favourite drinks of liquorice water and sweetly fizzy home-made lemonade. Sherry was her favoured tipple, which she indulged in mainly on social occasions.

Her appreciation of the simple, dorm-feast type of food gave her the capacity to convey with flair and style the mouth-watering tea parties (both designed and illicit) in which William and his associates participated. Cream buns and jellies and ice creams were often used as psychological weapons in the stories; on several occasions William worsts his principal enemies – the plump and greedy Hubert Lane and his gang – by contriving to seize and devour the goodies that have been lovingly laid out by Hubert's mother or one of his devoted aunts for the delectation of the Laneites. Tea-party food was also used as a weapon of vengeance in one of Richmal's wartime William books. In this episode Violet Elizabeth has a party which offers ices and cakes in pre-war proportions. William and co. are exhorted to save some of these for the deprived evacuee children who have come to their village but they fall on the feast with furious dedication, and mop up the last crumb. This is because the local children have suffered at the hands of 'the tough young guys from London' and are determined that their tormentors will not share their gastronomic treat. One of William's regular career ambitions (which alternates with his aspirations to be an engine-driver, a chimney sweep or a tramp) is to become a sweetshop owner when he grows up.

Richmal's brother Jack – the original inspiration of her dream child – had left the Rhodesian Mounted Police in 1919, but had chosen to remain in far-flung and colourful places. As an employee of a large merchant and shipping company, he worked and travelled a great deal in China. He had adventures there (including capture by bandits), as well as some earlier on in Africa which made spellbinding stories when he regaled his family with them during his leaves in England. There was always a room – 'Jack's room' – available at The Glebe, and Richmal looked forward to hearing his 'tallish travellers' tales'. Her home was enlivened further by various objects brought back from China and Africa, including some assegais (South African native spears) which were displayed on the landing.

It became obvious that Jack, whose unbookishness had once been the despair of his studious father, had at last developed a literary bent. For some time he had been helping Richmal by suggesting plots and situations for her William stories, and now, with 'glorious' real-life adventures of his own to inspire him, he wrote novels like *The White Kaffir* and *Trooper Fault*, which had African backgrounds. These appeared at the beginning of the thirties under the name of John Lambourne and were the forerunners of several stories of high and hectic adventure written by Jack. *Trooper Fault* received a Book Society recommendation, and excellent reviews from, amongst other newspapers, the *Birmingham Post* ('As good as Conan Doyle at his best') and *The Times* ('stirring ... vividly drawn characters and exciting episodes, including a wonderful fight'). There are echoes in Jack's literary success of William's stories and plays ('Dick of the Bloody Hand', etc.), which of course also featured men of action, and plenty of thrills and chills! Jack's books, however, were not just *Boy's Own Paper* stuff; like Richmal's, his stories were lit by flashes of wit and insight.

The titles of his African based novels *The Kingdom that Was* and its sequel *The Second Leopard, Strong Waters* and *The Unmeasured Place* suggest their mystery/adventure themes. The first two books mentioned convey a mood that is a cross between that of *Alice's Adventures in Wonderland* and Rider Haggard's *She*. Featuring intelligent, talking animals and lost, lush, time-shifted tropical worlds, these novels could be seen as Jack's more flamboyant interpretation of the secret-world motif which also intrigued Richmal.

Gwen, Richmal and Clara were thrilled by the success of their brother's books, and on his side Jack was proud of Richmal's achievements. Outside the family circle, however, he understandably preferred to play down his connection with William Brown, whose name was already becoming a generally recognized synonym for scruffy and belligerent boyhood. After resigning from the shipping company in 1932, Jack came home and lived at The Glebe for a while. Richmal would probably have been happy for him to stay permanently with Clara and herself, but Jack met and married a young widow, Joan Cooke.* They moved to Buckfastleigh in Devon, and then settled in Cornwall, where he took up a new career (of which William would also have approved): 'The study of insects had always been a hobby of mine ... I got down to it more earnestly – and fairly intense bee-keeping.' Jack and Joan had a son, David, in 1934 and a daughter, Sarah, ten years later. Richmal, already an aunt three

* There seems a rightness and an inevitability that Jack – who inspired William's creation – should marry a girl called Joan (see page 132).

times over with Gwen's children, was delighted to have a further nephew and niece.

During this period, Richmal was extremely productive as a writer. As she said of Bridget in *The Innermost Room*, 'she had two selves, one ordinary, one writing'. The strong thread of domesticity and family responsibility that ran through Richmal's life was something that she never resented. Friends like Joan Braunholtz have commented that, although her literary work must have been very demanding, she spoke far less about it than of her family: 'for her, home and family were all in all'. Richmal's interest in Gwen's children, Tommy, Margaret and Richmal, remained a major factor in her life. By the early 1930s Tommy Disher was well into his teens, away at boarding-school (Cheltenham College) and still providing Richmal with occasional stimulus for William exploits.

Richmal Ashbee, Tom's younger sister, is anxious to point out that William and other fictional characterizations owed far more to her aunt's considerable imaginative powers than to real-life personalities: 'Not very much of William seems to me to be based on anybody else. *Episodes* from her brother Jack's child-hood, I think she said she had used in the early stories, and again it would be *episodes* from my brother, Tom Disher's. There is a world of difference between a character and an episode.' One episode that Richmal Ashbee remembers Gwen telling her about was Tommy's keeping a stag-beetle in his underwear drawer, and feeding it with marmalade, which of course seeped into his things. Such an incident seemed ready-made for William, and Richmal Crompton wasted no time in fictionalizing it in *Still William*:

> William was, as not infrequently, under a cloud. His mother had gone to put some socks into one of his bedroom drawers and had found that most of the drawer space was occupied by insects of various kinds, including a large stag-beetle, and that along the side of the drawer was their larder, consisting of crumbly bits of bread and a little pool of marmalade.

William, who claims to be teaching the stag-beetle tricks, explains that it actually *does* eat the marmalade, because this gets less each day. His mother, somewhat acerbically, points out that the marmalade is simply soaking into the wood, to say nothing of his socks and hankies.

After her divorce in 1935, Gwen, who remained remarkably self-contained despite the stresses of her relationship with Disher, gave private coaching in maths to a few pupils at her home in Cumberland Road. Apart from sometimes helping Gwen's younger daughter with Latin, Richmal gave up teaching or coaching soon after she had been forced by her disablement to leave Bromley High School. Now, of course, she knew that she could never again lead a physically energetic life. Just as when she had been forced to rest on a backboard as a child, she now had once again to enjoy physical activity vicariously through the characters in her stories. She was still able to cycle, after a fashion, and she bought a bicycling machine so that she could practise in the privacy of her own home, and keep as much movement as possible in her legs. Her life took on a new dimension, however, when she decided to learn to drive a car. This, of course, had to be converted to hand controls, and Richmal was determined to master this new and, for her, essential skill as soon as she possibly could. 'I may be a bigger fool than some of them, but I can't be a bigger fool than all of them,' she said, with reference to other potential drivers, and some who were already on the roads.

Her taste for theatrical entertainment was something else that had now to be expressed in a less active way; she could no longer be the mainstay of school or church drama groups, but William could continue to put on his plays, tableaux and 'human waxwork' shows in the old barn (even if he could hardly ever manage to extract from the local children who made up his audience the agreed admission charge of a penny or halfpenny). Some of William's theatrical performances were inspired by Richmal's juvenile experiences of acting with Gwen in a church hall in Bury in aid of the Waifs and Strays Society. William, however, seems always to have illusions of grandeur when he is involved in amateur dramatics, even when his role is tiny, or when he is assigned a backstage job. Coerced into helping with sound effects for a production by the local literary society, William hankers for the hero's part so strongly that, when he encounters a distinguished professional treader of the boards, he feels justified in speaking to him on equal terms:

'Do you know who I am?' [the stranger said majestically].
'No,' said William simply, 'an' I bet you don't know who I am either.'
'I am a very great actor,' said the man.
'So'm I,' said William promptly.

Village theatricals are also featured in some of her adult books, with varying degrees of hilarity. Richmal enjoyed visits to the professional theatre in London with Gwen, and, later, with her niece, Richmal. She was not especially musical, but had a taste for Gilbert and Sullivan, hated jazz, and liked to hear classical music on the radio.

Richmal enjoyed visiting central London, which could be reached from Bromley in about twenty minutes by train. She liked to meet friends for lunch at the Charing Cross Hotel, and to shop at the Army & Navy in Victoria Street, Debenham & Freebody's, and Woollands of Knightsbridge. She was a member of the writers' section of the Lyceum Club (where she sometimes stayed overnight), of PEN and of the Society of Authors. Although she attended only relatively few of the functions, she enjoyed meeting kindred spirits there and made several lasting friendships.

One Lyceum Club friend was L. C. Mott (who wrote as 'Clive Arden'). In a letter to Richmal Ashbee after Richmal Crompton's death, she recalled an act of generosity which, she considered, was typical. Towards the end of the thirties, L. C. Mott had been 'suddenly precipitated into a London bed-sitter', where she was 'living on a bean until another novel could be written'. She lunched with Richmal at the Lyceum Club, and afterwards, when lighting a cigarette, Richmal accidentally caught the tip of L. C. Mott's hat-veil with the flame of her lighter. The small, wispy veil literally went up in smoke, but its owner was not particularly worried as she still had the hat, which was intact. A few days later she received a note from Richmal, saying that she was enclosing cash for a new veil, and, knowing that her friend was undergoing temporary financial difficulties, she'd like her to keep the change. Richmal sent £10; a new veil at that time would have cost only one and sixpence (7½p).

Living locally, Richmal still had a lot of contact with 'old girls' from the Bromley High School. She numbered Miriam Place, Audrey Carr and Joan Braunholtz amongst her friends, but often in Bromley's busy High Street shopping area she would run into girls (or rather young women) whom she had once taught, but whose names and sometimes even whose faces she had temporarily forgotten. Concerned, as always, not to hurt anyone's feelings unnecessarily, she worked out one or two probing but friendly sentences – 'Are you still living in the same place?', 'And how are you all?', etc. – which she kept at the tip of her tongue. These sentences never failed to draw sufficient information to remind Richmal of their identities.

She managed to remain extremely mobile, in spite of her disability. In the mid-1930s, according to Richmal Ashbee, she drove 'a small, four square saloon – bigger than a Baby Austin'. Just before the beginning of the Second World War she bought a Rover, which she then had to stick to 'for the duration'. With her car and the use of a stick she managed to go almost everywhere she wanted. Miriam Place and Joan Braunholtz remember her as being 'always brave' about her physical problems. 'Sometimes she would be very awkward about certain movements, but she always made light of this . . . she never mentioned polio, except when she joked about being "clumsy" '.

Fashion was never a great factor in Richmal's life. Her taste in clothes, as in food, was simple and straightforward. Having no particular favourite colour, she wore light greyish tweeds in winter and flower-printed dresses in summer. Clara liked to wear *large* flower-prints; Richmal's were smaller, and these became progressively smaller in pattern after Clara died. Richmal was happy to let Clara give her sartorial advice, and she also consulted Gwen's daughter Margaret, who was to make a successful career in fashion, about her clothes.

Although her taste in clothes was quiet, Richmal liked to wear bright lipstick and rather dark face-powder. One of the most striking aspects of her appearance as a young woman was her hair, which she wore long throughout her twenties and thirties. There are suggestions in some of her stories that she might have had a mild hair fetish; certainly she had very definite feelings about the coiffures she felt would suit her various characters. William's sister Ethel has seductively red-gold hair which thrills her admirers and is appropriate for her flirtatious nature. In *The Wildings*, during the early days of their marriage, David 'knelt with his face in [Hero's] long dark hair and kissed it and worshipped it. "I love your hair Hero . . . it's so long and shiny." ' In the same novel, eighteen-year-old Stella's symbolic act of revolt (when her mother refuses to let her train for a career) is to have her hair bobbed. In at least three of Richmal's short stories for adults, a woman's hair is the focal point. In 'The Spanish Comb', a story in the collection *Mist*, Moira's long dark hair is lovingly described on more than one occasion as it falls extravagantly over her shoulders. Her husband gives her an antique Spanish comb, but when she wears this in her hair she is taken over by insane and inexplicable jealousy. In a story called 'Hair' which appeared in *A Monstrous Regiment* (1927), one of Richmal's heroines has 'lovely hair – great silken waves of gold that reach below her waist'. She spends a lot of time caring for this, loving its feel, fragrance and warmth, grudging none of the time and trouble that she has to spend on keeping it groomed and gleaming. She even enjoys occasionally sitting 'in the golden meshes of her hair' and experiencing 'the warm sympathy of the shining strands'.

> When she looked forward – as all girls do – to the lover that time would bring to her, she did not feel diffident or unworthy. She had not beauty of face or greatness of intellect but she had this beauty to lay at his feet, this unrivalled wonder of silken gold. She was proud of its beauty – yet not as though it were part of herself. There was no vanity in her pride. She had endowed it with a separate personality. She worshipped its beauty, caressing it as though it were her child or friend or lover . . .

This nameless heroine is 'painfully shy and introspective', and she falls heavily for a rather cold, and also nameless, young man. The story has an ironic twist. She has 'her glorious cloak of hair' shingled because she things he has a preference for that current fashion; then – too late – she realizes that he is not interested in her at all but is already engaged to someone else. 'His fiancée was not shingled. She had straight fair hair dressed low at the back of her head.' Shock, horror – and then sobs from 'the shorn head', of course.

A second story entitled 'Hair', which does not seem to be featured in Richmal's published collections, is also about a woman's superabundant crowning glory. This is in lower key than the other story of the same name. John loves his wife, Janey, and is attracted by her 'comical monkey-like little face, the kindness and humour of her brown eyes, her shyness and gentleness'. What he can't stand is what she regards as her 'one claim to beauty' – her 'thick, lustrous, auburn ... rippling gleaming waves'. These lie between John and Janey in bed at night like a chastity barrier, and as the years pass by the hair takes on 'a definite character of its own ... supercilious and arrogant and malicious'. The story has a happy ending, however. Janey fractures her right arm, and learns that she will never again be able to raise it above her shoulders. She talks tremulously of cutting off her long and heavy hair – but John, to his own surprise, takes on its brushing and washing and grooming and dressing; when he does so, he begins to feel for it 'something of the affection one feels for a fallen foe. He had had it at his mercy, and had dealt with it chivalrously and generously. It seemed to look up at him in a grateful, humble, deprecating fashion. Gone was its arrogance, its sneering superciliousness. He knew that the three of them would get on very well together in the future!'

In *William*, Richmal writes that 'no woman can resist a man with yellow curls'; of course we know that she really means the exact opposite, and the characters upon whom she foists blond and bubbly coiffures are at best complacent and, at worst, downright dreadful. Bert is a slimy charmer who dons a yellow wig to try to ensnare the affections of a fairly well-off widow. As this lady is the sister of Mrs Roundelay – one of William's few adult friends, who keeps him regularly supplied with home-made gingerbread cookie-boys – he has to take the matter in hand and unmask (or rather unwig) the odious Bert.

Richmal's apparent antipathy to very blond men makes one wonder whether such a real-life man or boy had ever treated her rather badly. It has been suggested that she felt rather cool about one of her father's long-ago 'daily boarders', who, apparently, inspired the creation of a hypocritical, fair-haired man in *Anne Morrison*. It seems strange for someone as balanced as Richmal to project a childish dislike into so many of her books, but all those terribly twee children in the William stories tended to be blond curly-tops.

Richmal had started to smoke before the First World War, at a time when smoking for women was frowned upon (not because of anticipated health hazards, but because it was considered 'unwomanly'). Joan Braunholtz remembers that 'she smoked when few women did' – which could not have endeared Richmal to her non-smoking, non-drinking brother-in-law, Thomas Disher. Once when Richmal went to tea with Joan, the latter's father challenged her about her smoking. Richmal – almost as one of the feminine stereotypes in her books might have done – disarmingly replied: 'But being more fragile, surely we need more soothing.' She did, at one time, try to break her habit of smoking cigarettes – by puffing cigars.

Clara, although now obviously becoming older, was still extremely energetic and resourceful. She had been one of the founders of the Bromley Common branch of the Women's Institute (in the 1920s), and her interest in this never abated. She remained outgoing and lively, and, in the view of her grand-daughter Richmal Ashbee, distinctly dominating. However, she says that neither Gwen nor Richmal Crompton found her so; to them Clara remained 'marvellous'.

Aspects of David Wilding's mother seem to have derived from Clara. *The Wildings* was published in 1925, not so long after Richmal had been stricken with polio, and, of course, nursed by her mother. Mrs Wilding – who is also a dominating character – takes on the nursing of her small grandson when he has severe pneumonia, as well as having to look after one or two other invalids in the family at the same time. When David returns from London to Boltwood (Bury?) to give moral support during this family crisis, he finds his mother, as always, coping superbly. (This was long before the advent of antibiotics, when pneumonia and even the less serious conditions of bronchitis or influenza were likely to be killers.) David is worried in case the strain will be too much for his mother, but:

... her vigils and confinement to the house seemed to make no difference to her. She had betrayed no signs of anxiety even when Jackie's life was despaired of. She looked as handsome, as healthy, as regal, as carefully dressed and coiffured as ever. She was a mystery – a magnificent mystery, thought David.

And it seems likely that Richmal too thought that of her own mother. Clara had to nurse her younger daughter not only through poliomyelitis but also through the ravages of another grave illness, when it was found that Richmal had developed breast cancer. She had a mastectomy (which was apparently and surprisingly performed in her own home), and, as always, Clara capably took charge of the situation and looked after her. (Clara too had suffered from breast cancer.)

It says a great deal for Richmal's resilience that she coped with polio when she was in her thirties, and cancer in her forties, and that neither condition seems to have been allowed to disrupt her life too drastically. Perhaps it is trite to say that despite these personal tragedies she continued to write exuberant and entertaining books, and to live a full and happy life – but this seems an accurate assessment of the situation. She did not discuss her problems a great deal with friends or members of her family, although she was always ready to listen to their difficulties and to offer whatever help she could. Throughout her life she remained a staunch Christian and a practising member of the Church of England (even though she became interested in a more mystical approach to religious matters in the years before her death at the end of the 1960s). There is no doubt that she derived strength and stability from her religious beliefs when she knew that she was suffering from cancer, a condition that was dreaded far more in the thirties than it is now, when there is more hope of cure.

There was companionship between Clara and Richmal, as well as a strong mother–daughter relationship. Like so many of the women in Richmal's novels, they sat together in the evening doing their needlework in an almost late-Victorian manner. (In fact, this was probably a hangover from their home life together in Bury.) Their particular forte was canvas tapestry work (for firescreens, stool covers, etc.), in which Richmal carried out the finer stitching. Clara tended to tackle the bolder projects, like the making of rugs. She was also a keen sock knitter. As well as making these for the family she used to help a hard-up neighbour by paying her to knit them too, and, during the Second World War, to make sea-boot stockings for deep sea fishermen.

No one can read the William books for long without becoming aware of the prominence of sock mending (if not actually sock making) in the saga. It is, in fact, William's mother's main function. She is a placid lady who always concurs with her husband's opinions, automatically reiterating 'Yes dear' as she constantly darns – even after the arrival of nylon – the socks of her menfolk. In one of the books there is mention of her darning on no less than five different pages. She remains utterly unruffled by national or global crises so long as she can put needle to sock:

> Mr Brown's political views were always very violent.
> 'He's ruining the country ... I tell you he's bleeding the country to death. He ought to be hung for murder. That man's policy, I tell you, is wicked – *criminal*. Leave him alone and in ten years' time he'll have wiped out half the population of England by slow starvation. He's killing trade. He's *ruining* the country.'
> 'Yes, dear,' murmured Mrs Brown, 'I'm sure you're right – I think these blue socks of yours are almost done, don't you?'

She remains similarly serene when William (or Robert or Ethel) confides to her the desperate anguishes of their current personal predicaments:

> Mrs. Brown calmly cut off her darning wool as she spoke, and took another sock from the pile by her chair ...

It is at times a wonder that the maddeningly calm Mrs Brown has never been strangled with her own darning wool by an infuriated member of her family.

The sock-mending syndrome is equally in evidence in Richmal's adult stories. In *Anne Morrison*, for example, there is an early reference to a visit from a great-aunt who is very disagreeable, but who nevertheless knows the proper function of an elderly, unmarried lady:

> Aunt Susannah sniffed, and said that she supposed there was a mountain of undarned stockings as usual, and she might as well begin on them.

In the same episode the young Anne is expected to do something 'useful' – that is to say, to 'sew or knit' – and great-aunt Susannah is outraged when Anne timidly asks if she might read instead. (In fairness to Richmal, it should be pointed out that there is narrative support for Anne rather than stuffy great-aunt Susannah at this point.)

Richmal's ideal domestic menage did not include cats and dogs. Pets tended, however, to get foisted on to her. In the 1940s, for example, Jack's wife Joan acquired a Pekingese called Ming, but once their daughter Sarah was born she felt that the dog was becoming jealous of the new baby, and might hurt her. Richmal, despite not being a dog-lover, took Ming off Joan and Jack's hands. The peke brought a new element into her mistress's life, and for the next six years they were happy companions at The Glebe. Richmal walked more because of Ming, and of course the dog was content to walk at Richmal's fairly slow pace.

It is interesting that in her books small dogs like pekes and poms are not featured sympathetically. In *Felicity Stands By*, when the heroine goes to visit an old school friend, she finds an overfed and yapping pom in her house. Worse still, its middle-aged owner addresses it in doggy baby talk. In *William the Pirate*, Emmeline, an object of Robert's affections, has a pom that goes into paroxysms of fury over trifling matters, and whose tetchiness complicates the courting process. There is a further pernicious dog of the same breed in *Felicity Stands By* (this one belongs to a dreadful aunt who is described by her nephew as 'Mussolini and Bluebeard and Lenin and Nero and Lucrezia Borgia all rolled into one'). The pom, who is plaintive, whiny, 'asthmatic, corpulent, dyspeptic and generally revolting-looking', seems a suitable dog for its unpleasant owner (who is also, by the way, 'Secretary of a Total Abstinence Society, and an Anti-Swearing Society, and an Anti-Smoking Society, and an Anti-Dancing Society'). Does one catch a note here of Richmal's dislike for the non-smoking, non-drinking Thomas Disher? Both in the William books and in *Felicity Stands By* she makes a point occasionally of inflicting humiliation and inconvenience on various fictional total abstainers who are trying to convince the world – or at least the inhabitants of one small English village – of the rightness of their cause.

Richmal's rather negative attitude to poms and pekes in her stories, to the extent of having a particularly unfortunate Pekingese die of overeating, is a little baffling in view of her sympathetic manner of writing about William's relationship with Jumble: she describes the latter, however, as 'eager, playful, adoring – a mongrel unashamed – all sorts of a dog'. Perhaps this is the clue to her apparent antipathy towards poms, pekes and other small thoroughbreds: one of Jumble's greatest charms is that he *is* a mongrel and, even though fate ironically and unexpectedly thrust a pedigree peke into Richmal's arms, part of her still mistrusted dogs which had had just a bit too much breeding. (Richard Ashbee comments: 'Mongrelness would not matter, nor pedigree. Pamperedness would.')

Although she wrote both entertainingly and touchingly about dogs, Richmal was not a 'doggy' person; neither was she – in any sense of the word – a 'catty' one. She seems to have felt little enthusiasm for cats. Neither, of course, does William. In the course of his career he inadvertently kills two felines (with little show of remorse) and maddens several others, in company with their owners. From time to time, different moggies supposed to belong to the Brown family are mentioned in the books. One, together with her kitten, has no name but is described as being William's 'inveterate enemy'. On another occasion the Browns own a short-tempered cat called Smuts, who also cherishes a dire hatred of William; and yet another pussy on the Browns' domestic hearth (this time one called Terence) 'dislikes William intensely'. The only cat who is represented in the stories with any sympathy is that belonging to the next-door neighbour, an animal which William uses for pebble-throwing target practice from time to time. We are told that this rather dim creature always looks upon William's pebble throwing as a sign of affection, and purrs loudly in response.

Richmal makes a point of mocking the extremely intense feelings that many people have for their cats. In *William the Gangster*, for example, when William is (reluctantly) staying with his Aunt Florence, he decides to while away a boring afternoon by teaching Smut, her pampered black puss, to do some ratting. Furious at being unceremoniously thrust head first into several rat-holes, the unco-operative feline escapes William's grasp and streaks off. Demented by Smut's absence, Aunt Florence begins to suspect William's involvement in his defection; so William 'borrows' Smu – another over-indulged black cat and Smut's deadly rival in all the local cat competitions. Plying the apparently returned prodigal with sardines and cream, Aunt Florence doesn't realise that the switch has taken place, even though she has constantly told William previously that Smut is *far* more handsome and impressive than Smu.

The Glebe was very much a reflection of Richmal and her tastes. She had acquired a few pieces of late 18th and early 19th Century furniture (some real, some good imitation) which with glasses, china and engravings of the period she used to excellent effect in creating an atmosphere of dignity and well being. On the walls she had old topographical prints, Rowlandson pictures, classical allegorical scenes, 19th Century fashion plates and some Baxter prints of Victorian buildings. Exotic touches were provided in her fine Persian blue sitting-room carpet, and Jack's gifts to her, from his travels, of laquered Chinese bowls and boxes, and embroidered hangings.

However, she also responded to the simplicity and strength of Dürer prints, and one of her most cherished pictures was a large reproduction of Giotto's *St Francis and the Birds* which hung in her study, together with a full colour original picture of William, which was given to her by Thomas Henry.

As well as having many pictures on the walls of The Glebe, Richmal enjoyed art from books, and was particularly fascinated by the work of Stanley Spencer and Samuel Palmer. She collected books of reproductions of the work of many artists, liking to study these as well as attending exhibitions – an activity which, because of her disablement, was not always easy for her. She had a taste for medieval narrative paintings (and used to send postcard prints of these to her friends at Christmas time long before art galleries began to make them into formal greetings cards).

Richmal's feelings for houses are persuasively expressed in her novels and short stories. For example, in every one of the stories of the supernatural in *Mist*, a home or garden plays a prominent part; there is Bletchleys, a sinister and ungainly old residence with an ancient oak in the garden that is supposed to date back to the Druids who worshipped trees of this kind; there is a 'stately' country house; a family home that 'hates' its new owners; and a delectable garden which provides the setting for a daunting story of someone 'possessed'. Her 1926 novel *The House* (published in the United States under the more apt title of *Dread Dwelling*) also concentrates on the macabre mood of a home; in *Frost at Morning* there is 'a room giving up for lack of encouragement'; in *The Gypsy's Baby* there are lovingly detailed descriptions of diverse interiors from rambling vicarages to cramped cottages and mellow farm-houses. Several other novels feature lush country gardens and cosy Victorian domestic settings.

Gardens and gardening are used as therapy (as, in *The Camel's Hump*, digging is exploited by Kipling as a cure for bad temper). In *Felicity Stands By*, a Mrs Fanning is 'a chronic invalid', and lively young Felicity knows how to work the miracle of her cure. She rather tortuously diverts Mrs Fanning's yearning for a 'psychic experience' into a grim determination to take a lot of physical exercise, and gardening is seen as particularly health-building: 'Always till now Mrs Fanning had been a stranger to good bouts of hard digging lasting for several hours.' It is reassuring to hear that, after Felicity's tough and stringent attentions, Mrs Fanning finds herself 'bathed in the delicious sense of weariness that only a day's hard exercise can bring'.

The Glebe housed several hundred books in polished book-cases. Books held a lifelong fascination for Richmal, who was an avid reader as well as a dedicated writer. The range of books which she enjoyed was truly vast, extending from Victorian boys' school stories and domestic tales to Homer and Horace, with many different strands in between. In childhood, as well as constantly creating her own stories and poems, she liked to read fiction by Mrs Ewing, Edith Nesbit and Lewis Carroll, and she loved fairy stories. When writing as an adult she liked to bring references to her favourite works – Francis Thompson's 'The Hound of Heaven', Tennyson's *Idylls of the King*, etc. – into her stories. She was an enthusiastic reader of Jane Austen, Dickens, Hardy and Trollope. Of twentieth-century novelists she admired Aldous Huxley, and, although she didn't find Evelyn Waugh quite so palatable, she was impressed by his precise use of words. Irish Murdoch's books, however, were given a wide berth, because Richmal found them 'too complicated'.

She was intrigued by the Brontës, and late in her life wrote to Joan Braunholtz: 'I've been reading a collection of Brontë letters. They so very nearly got their little school going. It would have been fun to have been a child in it if they had.'

She also often mentioned ephemeral writings in her stories. In *Anne Morrison*, for example, when Anne is travelling to 'the school known as The Priory', she reads on the train the popular children's magazine *Little Folks*. Once at the school, her elder sister, Lorna, reads the serial story 'The King's Flag' (doubtless an authentic one) from the *Girl's Own Paper*. Richmal liked to read several novels at once. She would always keep a volume of Dickens to re-read in the car, in case at any time she had to wait in it; whatever 'serious' reading matter she was tackling was usually available in the sitting-room at The Glebe, and she made sure that 'something light' (perhaps a detective story) was kept in her bedroom. She once commented rather ruefully: 'Sometimes the plots became confused.'

There could easily have been a tendency for her own plots to become confused, as well. She wrote notes for plots on the backs of used envelopes, old letters and small scraps of paper (and very probably also on the back of the proverbial bus ticket). These could be found all round her house, and sometimes there were many different versions of the same sentence, theme, conversation or incident. Occasionally she used notebooks – but these tended simply to become stuffed-out receptacles for the pieces of paper to which she committed her fast-moving thoughts.

Richmal sometimes clipped these snippets together under headings such as 'Children', 'Historical', 'Family'. A random dip into a bunch of these brings up items like the following:

Children Theme

Richmal D: 'I'm busy, Don't intersturb me.'
'He was eaten by an antelator.'
'It's delicious but I don't like it.'

Family   Elderly widow had mean husband who grudged her every penny and wouldn't let her entertain at all. He died, leaving her £48,000. She said simply, 'It's so lovely to be able to do what I like.'

Relationships

Bullying companion-help. Uses power unmercifully ('Shut up', etc.) – loud, angry, bawling voice – but very efficient. Home well run – old lady's comfort considered (but any rebellion punished by neglect of her comfort)...

Richmal had an astonishing capacity to conjure from these scrappy notes her gleeful William books and serious family sagas. She usually confined her time for writing to mornings only, and wrote her books in longhand before they were typed. (She had help from a professional typist, who charged extra because Richmal's writing was so appalling. However, during the war this help was unavailable, and Richmal then took to doing her own typing.)

Richmal Ashbee remembers her aunt being secretive about her writing, and only letting her family read things when they were quite finished, but her daughter Kate recalls that when she and her brother Edward were little her great-aunt would read them William snippets hot from the typewriter. Richmal Crompton certainly tried to keep her writing fairly secret during her childhood, and her reticence about her stories and poems is echoed in *The Innermost Room*, when Bridget, at fifteen years of age, is

composing little stories and poems that she wrote alone in a little writing-case that Derek her brother had given her.

No-one knew of their existence except herself. She was in some curious way both proud and ashamed of them. She felt she would have died in torture rather than show one to anyone.

William, as a reader, had very definite ideas on what makes people buy and want to read books:

> If ever I write a book I'm goin' to have a picture of a big splash of blood on the back . . . It'd make anyone want to read it . . . they know it would be a nice excitin' one . . . It's 'str'ordin'ry to me to see books like what one sees with girls' faces and such-like on the back. Who'd want to read a book with a girl's face on the back? Anyone sens'ble would sooner read about a murder than a girl any day . . .

William likes to read (and write) ghost stories of the lurid variety, with luminous skeletons, rattling chains, secret passages and hidden treasure. Unlike his verbal story-telling, his writing is not fluent. On one occasion, when the Outlaws have to compose a circular advertising the 'Wembley Exhibition' that they are to stage in the old barn (admission one penny), they find the process of creative writing 'physically and mentally exhausting: . . . they could run and wrestle and climb trees all day without feeling any effects, but one page of writing always had the peculiar effect of exhausting their strength and spirit!' These efforts at literary creation involved William in heavy frowning, and in sticking his tongue out as he concentrated. He wrote, apparently, in an illegible hand that sloped dizzily across the page, using 'orthography that was the despair of his teachers'. His language, of course, makes liberal use of melodramatic exclamations, like 'Gadzooks!', 'Methinks!', and so on, and his sub-literary compositions are generally variations on the hero-of-the-bloody-hand theme. Richmal seems with these to be parodying both the bloody and thunderous pulp paper stories and the more respectable, but similarly inflated, hard-backed historical adventures that many boys devoured during the late-Victorian and Edwardian periods. Articles which she wrote about early children's stories sharply point their melodramatic plots (horrible accidents overtaking boys and girls who have disobeyed their elders, etc.). With her strongly developed sense of history, she would surely also have reacted against the anachronistic epics of G. A. Henty and his imitators. In the world of boys' fiction, school stories appealed to her rather more than swashbuckling adventures or 'fancy-dress' historical tales, and she admired the story-telling skills of Charles Hamilton ('Frank Richards'), who produced the long-running sagas of Greyfriars School in the *Magnet* and St. Jim's in the *Gem*.

When William is in one of his cynical moods, he says furiously that he doesn't think 'there's a single book that needs to have been printed'. Richmal would have agreed with him as far as the 'deeply psychological novel' was concerned. In *Enter – Patricia*, someone is reading one of these, in which 'the hero's every thought was dissected at length. Nothing happened. It was the sort of book which publishers call "brilliantly analytical" '.

Richmal took the business of reading and writing seriously. She regularly collected reviews, and kept long lists of the books that she wanted to read. Some she bought, and some she borrowed. (She used to get books on loan from both Boots and the public libraries in Bromley; once she and her niece, Richmal Ashbee, found themselves vying with each other through the local library system for an elusive copy of Tolkien's *The Lord of the Rings*.) Richmal was sometimes asked to open children's sections in these libraries; on one occasion, the local librarian proudly described her to the audience as 'a borrower', with such emphasis that Richmal commented afterwards that it made her feel about three inches tall (like one of the miniaturized characters in Mary Norton's popular juvenile book *The Borrowers*).

Richmal often sends up what she called 'second-rate literature' in her books, as well as what might be termed 'third-rate authors'. She has a great deal of fun in debunking a particularly pretentious one in *Frost at Morning*. Mrs Sanders, who is the rather colourful wife of a vicar, achieves a lot of success with her (very) light novels, but is slipshod. In a book on which she is working, being unable to read her own writing she has difficulty in understanding one particular word. She decides that it could be 'hyena' – or 'hyacinth' – or even 'hymnal' (the logic and flow of her narrative give her no more clues than this). The puzzling word eventually turns out to be 'hymen'. She also has to seek an alternative to 'ecstasy' in the thesaurus, because 'I've used it three times in this paragraph. No, four.'

Mrs Sanders works on several books at once and sometimes mixes them up. She performs her acts of literary creation in a state of total confusion, unlike Richmal, who was always extraordinarily well organized inwardly, even though externally all those scraps of paper in scribbly handwriting might have seemed to suggest disorder. Poor Mrs Sanders! She is so wrapped up in her writing that she can barely recognize her own child if she passes her in the corridor of their straggling vicarage home; but 'slowly, surely, incredibly', her sales began to shrink'. Then she has nothing left.

Amongst her papers, Richmal kept several quotations from what various authors (R. L. Stevenson, D. H. Lawrence, W. Somerset Maugham and Phyllis Bentley, among others) had written concerning books and authorship. When asked to produce an article about writing children's books, she said she felt like 'a wolf in sheep's clothing', because originally her William stories were for adults. She commented that 'children enjoy assimilating new facts and ideas only if the author is willing to rediscover these with the children ... You must be able to see the world as the child sees it. To "write down" is an insult that the child quickly perceives.'

When Richmal died in 1969 she left a list of some thirty books that she had still wanted to acquire and read. This included several books on mysticism, volumes of poetry, biographies (from George Eliot to Osbert Lancaster) and works of fiction (by Brigid Brophy, Radclyffe Hall, Muriel Spark and Elizabeth Taylor). Her choice of books reflected her multilayered, open and inquiring personality.

She left her extremely large personal library to Richmal Ashbee's husband, Paul, who has kept her collection of books intact. As well as exploring her secret worlds, Richmal had nurtured a passion for foreign travel ever since her childhood days. Her inquiring mind and lively imagination were stirred by Edward's stories about faraway places, and her fascination with these was echoed by the fictional Anne Morrison who, as a small girl, pored over illustrated travel books in her father's study:

There was another book that Anne looked at again and again. She loved the pictures in that one. They were pictures of places very brightly coloured. There was Egypt, with very golden sands and a very blue sky ... there was Japan, with bright pink blossom against another very blue sky ... there was Sicily, gleaming gold and white narcissi ... fields of them ... and there were ever so many more ... just like fairy places ... places you couldn't imagine were real, but they were real, and rich people could go to see them. They were there — all blue and gold and flowers and sunshine — somewhere, at exactly the same time that Anne was sitting on the study hearthrug looking at their pictures, and it was that that made them so thrilling.

Anne's travel ambitions were to be fulfilled at the end of the novel because, unmarried at thirty, lonely, but 'still the "captain of her soul, the master of her fate" ', she receives an unexpected legacy of ten thousand pounds which brings Sicily, Greece, Egypt, and even Japan easily within her reach.

The real-life Richmal was less fortunate. When she was young and fit, she had neither the time nor the money for extensive travel (and of course for four years of her youth the Great War had drastically curtailed foreign holidays). Later on, when she had achieved affluence through her writing, she was too disabled to undertake very long or arduous trips abroad. She never travelled further afield than Europe, and even there didn't get as far as Greece, which in view of her passion for classics would surely have been her principal travel target.

Over the years she built up, and kept until she died, a wad of picture postcards which she had received from friends and relatives when they were on holiday in various parts of Britain or elsewhere. She had none of the antipathy towards holidays that afflicted her most popular hero, who, we are told, was 'much relieved that his family was not taking a holiday (for William hated to be torn from his familiar pursuits and the familiar fields and ditches of his native village)'. And, in another of the books:

> ... he hated being dragged from his well-known haunts, his woods and fields and dog (for Jumble was not the sort of dog

one takes away on a holiday)... [William] hated the
uncongenial atmosphere of hotels and boarding houses ...
He took a pride and pleasure in the expression of gloom and
boredom that he generally managed to maintain during the
whole length of the holiday.

The Brown family, on the other hand, were always trying to get
William to go away, so that at least for a brief period peace and
tranquillity might reign at their home: in *William the Pirate* Ethel
remarks fervently, 'Wouldn't it be *heavenly* if someone would
ask William somewhere for even a week?'

Richmal kept journals (or at least detailed notes) of several of
her foreign holidays as well as pre-holiday planning notebooks.
The places she is known to have visited are Italy and France in
1924 (surely a strenuous travel programme so soon after her
recovery from polio), Oberammagau at some time before the
Second World War, Iceland and Scandinavia in 1939, Denmark
and Sweden in 1947, Italy again in 1952 and 1962, and Germany
in 1963. There might well have been other trips abroad of which
she didn't keep a journal, or of which her notes have been lost.
Her disability permitted her, according to Paul Ashbee, to walk
in a 'spritely enough' way round historic houses, galleries and
other places of interest so long as she occasionally had
someone's arm as a support, and didn't remain on her feet for
too long.

Her 1924 trip to Italy was made in company with Decima
Leek, the French mistress at Bromley High School, and
Richmal's diary of the holiday suggests that it fulfilled her high
expectations. Even before she arrived in Boulogne ('Lovely
crossing – sea deep blue, dappled by the sun') she seemed
enraptured. She and her companion travelled by train across
France to Italy; on the way she noted that 'whole families were
working in the fields – old women especially', and that the faded
white houses looked as if they had grown from the fields. 'The
bustle of Paris', however, impressed her more than the
picturesque activities of the French peasants. She found that the
'carefree atmosphere' was 'like a tonic', the waitresses in the
cafes and bars were 'cheery', and the customers were 'vivacious,
chattering and laughing'. This expansive, glowing mood is

sustained throughout the long journey, during which she was captivated by the panoramic views of 'blue lakes, pines tall and straight, deep grey-blue mountains', and so on.

On reaching Venice, Richmal diligently visited St Mark's and the Doges' Palace, went in a gondola, had tea at Florian's, and took a steamer to the islands and the Lido. People, in fact, impressed her rather more than canals and buildings, and she enjoyed sitting on the Piazza 'watching the crowd – priests, soldiers, Parisians, Americans, English, Venetians in their graceful scarves, monks, etc.'.

Florence ('a rush of trams; continual honking of horns') impresses her less than Venice. She catalogues the art treasures that she is able to see there, and keeps an eye on the natural scene.

Driven by horse cab to Fiesole, she admires the wonderful views of cypresses, irises, wisteria, lilacs, roses and almond trees in blossom. At the monastery she admires the blaze of flowers, and the fresco of *St Francis and the Birds*. She sees Michelangelo's cell, with his pencil sketches on the wall, and is intrigued when one of the monks says, 'I wish you a good time – and a good time in paradise.' Later she sees and is much moved by Donatello's *Annunciation* – 'graceful shrinking little Madonna, hand at breast, looking not at angel but as if into distance'. Giotto's cloister frescoes impress her, and, at San Marco, Fra Angelico's 'lovely frescoes in cells, Ghirlandaoi's Last Supper', etc. Everything is enhanced by the 'glorious views of the Apennines all round . . .'.

Richmal's journal then describes a 'curious incident', which appears to have taken place somewhere on this drive. After sitting for an hour in a church, savouring the 'peace and calm and immensity', she came out into a sudden thunderstorm. She writes that she 'sheltered . . . and told man address'. (There is no clue to this man's identity.) 'He sat on, and so did I – after about five minutes he told me that he was engaged and thought I only wanted to shelter from rain'. Her holiday notes do not remain long in this enigmatic mood. She travels on to Rome, where she visits the Forum and drives along the Appian Way, where she sees mulecarts from the country decorated with 'gay red woollen tassels and fringes and innumerable bells'. She writes at length about these mules, and the crowds of 'happy peasants'.

Visiting the Catacombs, she 'did not go down, except the first flight', and another reminder of her disability comes when 'the lame ticket clippie at Villa d'Este made me have his chair, and refused a tip'.

At St Peter's she is moved by the 'lovely Pieta of Michel Angelo' though considers that it 'would be better without gilt additions. The whole effect is too much gilt and inlaid marble – magnificent but not restful, not "dim or religious" enough'. Similarly, at the Vatican she admires the 'magnificent guards' and the 'lovely' Sistine Chapel but is not impressed by Raphael's room: 'Raphael not at his best in made-to-order historical scenes to glorify his hirers'.

At Naples and Pompeii she seems less interested in the ruins than in the contemporary inhabitants, 'swarthy . . . dirty and happy-looking men and women, working in gardens . . .' and often she comments on the children who come 'running up to beg'.

How she and Decima fared as travelling companions is not detailed, but a terse entry 'Decima went to Capri. I not', suggests that there were times when each was glad to be on her own. (Possibly too Richmal found some of their joint sight-seeing physically over-arduous.) She went alone to San Martino, which she had difficulty in finding, and the expedition was further marred, as she went round the church, 'by the beastly and amorous guide who insisted on placing me in best position for each picture, with a lot of mauling and pawing. Couldn't do anything in circs. but grin and bear it.' Happily this romantic byplay didn't entirely spoil her enjoyment of 'the beautifully inlaid wood on monks' stalls, the altar of amethyst and agate and lapis lazuli and sandstone', or of the Veronese painting there.

Richmal visited a cameo factory, and on her way back to her hotel by taxi, 'passed by some dreadful hovels'. She was intrigued by the workmen who sat at the side of the road, eating long rolls 'almost as big as umbrellas, cut open and made into sandwiches'.

Pisa produces no mention of the leaning tower but simply the short comment 'town itself unattractive but nice bookshop'.

Her visit to Italy ends on a high note with a wonderful train journey to Lugano, and spectacular scenery around the lake.

(Characteristically, however, she is as much impressed by the human element as by the natural grandeur.) 'Blue lake among blue hills in front of ... range upon range of snow-capped mountains against blue sky ... fascinating little villages by the side of the lake; women washing clothes by the lake-side, kneeling by sloping scrubbing boards.'

There was about this and her trip to France in the same year (when she was so moved by her experience in Sacré-Coeur – see page 60) a sense of 'that first, fine careless rapture' that she might never quite recapture. Her records of later European holidays are less detailed, and slightly less refulgent, but all of them provided stimulus and settings for her literary creations.

In 1939 she had planned a trip to the Baltic but, because of the uncertainty of the international situation, this was put off in favour of a cruise of the Scandinavian fjords. Richmal's travelling companions on her trips abroad included Elsie Wilmore (her friend from Royal Holloway College), and Elsie's companion, Charlotte; Richmal Ashbee accompanied her aunt on several holidays abroad and in Britain. Despite her disability, Richmal Crompton enjoyed travelling and, in particular, flying. She continued to take the occasional trip abroad until the mid-1960s, by which time her health was deteriorating and she was, of course, well into her seventies.

CHAPTER 7

PATRIOTISM, POLITICS AND PRECIOUS CAUSES

"They get ten shillin's a week for doin' nothin', while we work an' work an' work day after day."

The declaration of war between Britain and Germany on September 3rd 1939 signalled drastic changes in many people's lives. For Richmal and Gwen, bereavement and disruption had occurred earlier, in May, when Clara had died from a heart attack at the age of 77. Even during the last months of her life she had still been 'magnificent', looking after Richmal and the house, and doing a major cleaning up and clearing out job at The Glebe. She sensed that her time was running out and wanted to leave everything straight for Richmal. (She had suffered previous heart attacks.) The gap in Richmal's life – and Gwen's – seemed enormous. Of course, Jack missed her too, but living in Cornwall, and preoccupied with the concerns of his wife and young son, he was somewhat distanced from the full effects of his mother's death.

Gwen wasn't happy at the thought of Richmal living at The Glebe on her own after Clara died, and with the declaration of war and the threat of air raids on the home counties, she moved in with her sister. Of course, Gwen's daughters, Margaret and Richmal, joined the household too. This marked the beginning of even greater closeness than had existed previously between Richmal and her nieces. Tom Disher was already in the Territorials, and early in the war he went with the Royal Corps of Signals to the Western Desert. (A few years earlier, in the middle of the 1930s, he had joined the Royal Fusiliers, but then decided that he did not want to make a career in the regular army, and his aunt had bought him out.)

There was the flurry of filling sandbags and piling them against the house, and of erecting air-raid shelters. An Anderson outdoor shelter was brought over from the Cumberland Road house and erected in the garden of The Glebe. Bunks were installed in this, but Richmal soon decided that she would be more comfortable sleeping on a mattress under the stairs, so only Gwen and the younger Richmal slept in the Anderson. She remembers that attempts were made to convert her aunt's study into a gas-proof room, and also recalls that when Gwen and the two Richmals first tried on their gas masks Tommy (who was home on leave) and Richmal Crompton's maid roared with laughter at the sight. (This may have triggered off some of the incidents in the wartime William books: William was always rather resentful that his parents didn't allow him to use his gas mask as a prop in his extravagant games, and he remained convinced that grown-ups, when hidden from juvenile eyes, wore them to pop out at each other in bizarre variants of peep-bo.)

Bromley was in the path of the German bombers' run-in to London, and it was also – as the plane flies – very near to Biggin Hill, which was to become one of the Battle of Britain airfields. Air-raid precautions in the Bromley area were therefore taken quite seriously. Richmal decided that she would like to undertake some form of war service; of course, because of her paralysed leg, her options were limited. She was now in her fiftieth year, but prepared to take on a substantial job, even if her physical energy was restricted. She joined the Auxiliary Fire

Service (later the National Fire Service) in Bromley and was given the responsibility of coping with the branch's telephone calls. She used to get up at 5 a.m. in order to report for duty in time for her early shift at the fire station which had been established in the grounds of the Bromley County Grammar School for Boys.

Richmal remained in the Fire Service from 1939 until 1943. She then gave it up because the organization had become too rigid, and she was expected to keep leaping to her feet to salute an officious superior who was one of the local butchers. It is surely no co-incidence that William skirmishes with a bossy and beastly Section Officer of the Fire Service in *William Does His Bit* (1941), and of course gets the better of him. Richmal had effected a nifty literary revenge.

Happily, despite the demands of her wartime voluntary service, her writing went on, unabated. The *Happy Mag.*, like so many periodicals, ended suddenly in May 1940, after Hitler's invasion of Norway had cut off Britain's main supply of 'pulp' paper. Richmal continued to produce almost as many William stories as before, but these were now written to be put into books straight away, without prior publication in a magazine. Her adult novels also continued to appear regularly throughout the war.

Richmal did voluntary work 'for the duration' at the Toc H canteen for Service personnel, located first at Bromley Common and then at Keston. She enjoyed this very much and made long-lasting friendships with some of the service-men and women whom she met there. Her other contributions to the war effort were to become a blood-donor, and of course to continue to grow vegetables in the large garden at The Glebe. Meanwhile, Gwen had taken over the management of the household with the same cheerful efficiency that Clara had brought to the task, and Jack temporarily abandoned his bees and insects and joined the RAF as a pilot officer in Flying Control in 1940, and was later promoted to flight lieutenant. One of his postings was to Iceland where for a time he served under Air Commodore Cecil George Wigglesworth who had, according to William Amos in *The Originals: Who's Really Who in Fiction*, been one of the original inspirations for Captain W. E. Johns's Biggles. (It is intriguing but appropriate that a challenging wartime situation should bring together these real-life counterparts of two of the most addictive of boys' fiction heroes.)

During the war period, Richmal produced some of her sharpest and most entertaining stories in *William and the Evacuees, William Does His Bit* and *William Carries On*. Like real-life children all over the country, William collected scrap-iron for salvage, picked up pieces of shrapnel and fragments from fallen aircraft for souvenirs, and dreamed of catching a German spy. It was no surprise to his many admirers that he should shove a saucepan on his head as a makeshift steel helmet, and, using a tin tray as a shield, try to remove a suspected unexploded bomb from outside the home of a friend. What was surprising was that the frivolous and work-shy Ethel, after almost two decades of just sitting around and looking decorative, should actually take on a job. Three jobs in fact: she helps with ARP work, has a brief spell in the ATS and then becomes a VAD. The impact of the war on the Brown family is further demonstrated in the loss of their cook, who joins the ATS. They cling carefully to Emma, the housemaid who has been with them since the early days of the stories. It is interesting that Richmal also lost her daily maid during the war, when she left her work at The Glebe to become a bus conductress. For the rest of the war, and afterwards, Richmal had only very part-time domestic and gardening help. One other responsibility that she undertook at this time was the secretaryship of the local branch of the United Society for Christian Literature.

Despite the social shake-ups brought about by the war, before, during and after it Richmal remained, according to Joan Braunholtz, 'a true-blue Tory. You could say that she was a temperamental conservative.' Nevertheless the William books can often be seen as a challenging critique of Conservative values, and Richmal seems to enjoy poking fun at Tory (and other) politicians in several stories:

William was frankly bored. School always bored him. He disliked facts and he disliked being tied down to detail, and he disliked answering questions. As a politician a great future would have lain before him.

On one occasion the Outlaws decide to hold their own parliamentary election, and each of them has to represent one of the main political parties. In the light of Richmal's views, it is appropriate that William, the leader, should be the one to have Conservatism foisted upon him, and to become the elected prime minister. To redress the balance, however, he can also be found flirting with Bolshevism. In fact he becomes *the* member, the only member, of the junior branch of the Society of Reformed Bolshevists, because Robert and his friends (the Society of Advanced Bolshevists) are determined to keep William out of their grown-up political group. Therefore they make him into one all on his own. He is quite happy to be its president, secretary, committee and members because, like many a more celebrated politician, he is mainly interested in the sound of his own voice, so doesn't mind when the only audience he can address is the next-door neighbour's imperturbable puss:

'All gotter be equal,' he pronounced fiercely, 'all gotter have lots of money. All 'uman beings. That's *sense*, isn't it? Is it *sense* or isn't it?'

The cat from next door scratched its ear and slowly winked.

'Well, *then*,' said William, 'someone ought to *do* somethin'.'

And he does. He co-opts more members into the junior branch, and they appropriate the cameras, watches, walking sticks, etc., of their elder brothers (who represent the senior branch of the Bolshevists). It all backs up Richmal's conviction that Bolshevism or Communism can't work, but that Conservatism can. As a sadder and wiser Robert eventually explains to his father, 'It's all right when you can get your share of other people's things, but when other people try to get their share of your things, then it's different.'

If Bolshevism sits uneasily upon William, fascism suits him even less. The story 'William and the Nasties' was first published in the *Happy Mag.* in June 1934, arguably at a time when there was little awareness outside Hitler's Germany of the real meaning of Nazism. The story was included in the book *William the Detective* in 1935, but it is significant that both Richmal Crompton's literary executor, Richmal Ashbee, and

117

Macmillan, the publishers of the current reprints, unhesitatingly decided to drop this episode completely from new editions of the book.

The story was possibly triggered off by some fairly inconsequential bilingual wordplay:

'I'll be the chief one. What's he called in Germany?'

'Herr Hitler,' said Henry.

'Her!' echoed William in disgust. 'Is it a woman?'

And, of course, in keeping with his male-chauvinist principles, William appoints himself as 'Him' Hitler.

As 'Nasties', the Outlaws make up their minds to chase out the Jewish owner of the local sweetshop (who, they suspect, is giving them short measure), and to snaffle his stock. Even though Richmal might not then have realized the worst excesses of Nazism, she knew enough ('They've got people called storm troops an' when these Jews don't run away they knock 'em about till they do') to begin to find the episode unpalatable even before she had finished writing it. 'A strange distaste for the whole adventure' overtakes the Outlaws, and Richmal rapidly rolls up the ending. Mr Isaacs, the sweet-shop proprietor, is transmogrified from tight-fisted baddie to beaming benefactor, and the Outlaws, much relieved, abandon their anti-semitic activities.

How Richmal came to write this story is a mystery. Her patriotic feelings were not the type that would find expression through xenophobia, and generally speaking her books are without the touches of anti-semitism that crop up in many other popular stories of the 1920s and 30s. It is possible, of course, that she hoped simply to draw attention to the perniciousness of fascism, and that the story got out of hand but, needed for a *Happy Mag.* deadline, just had to be finished and sent off.

Although the Macmillan reprints are in the main faithful to the originals, a further episode, 'William and the League of Perfect Love' was also omitted from the 1985 edition of *William the Detective*. The discarding of these two stories, in each of which William's behaviour topples over from anarchism to callousness, suggests that children's book publishers today are motivated by greater sensitivity than some of their predecessors. (It should, however, be remembered that these stories were

118

originally published in an adult periodical. The collecting of the William stories into books for children was, as mentioned on page 68, a somewhat haphazard affair, which might not have reflected editorial attitudes towards juvenile books.)

As surely as she would have repudiated Nazism and everything it stood for, Richmal would have reacted vigorously against cruelty towards animals. Yet William engages in this in the second of these discarded tales, whose title – 'William and the League of Perfect Love' – hardly indicates the nature of its contents. William and Jumble are on one of their country 'walks' (William is actually crawling on his belly through several ditches, stalking an innocent passer-by whom he has decided is a spy; Jumble is hurling himself on sticks, stones and other contents of the ditch in one of his energetic but abortive rabbit-catching exercises.) They come to a farm-yard, which has an enclosure 'full of rats'. The man in charge explains that the fox-terrier belonging to the farm is to be put into the enclosure to kill off the rats (who have been caught and rounded up). William, forgetting his customary role as 'friend and protector of the rat tribe' urges the man to also let Jumble loose on the unfortunate rodents.

A competition is arranged to see which dog can kill the more rats within a given time. Details of the gory mutilations and murders that follow are not dwelt upon, although it is made clear that Jumble deals death and destruction on a large scale, to the accompaniment of William's 'frenzied yells' of encouragement and 'frantic joy' when his dog becomes the winner of the contest. This seems another strange example of a story which inexplicably got out of hand. It has already been pointed out that Richmal's attitude towards animals was not particularly sentimental, but this callous approach to violent, mass extermination is totally out of character.

Richmal supported several causes which were precious to her. In the course of a year she was likely to send donations to some twenty-five or thirty different charities. Several of these were Church and Christian groups, some were concerned with the welfare of children, and some with helping the disabled. (In 1947, for example, she made a BBC radio appeal on behalf of the then Infantile Paralysis Fellowship – now the British Polio

Fellowship – which raised the considerable sum of £4,070.) She was particularly supportive of the work of her cousin, Canon Robin Lamburn, who had worked for many years at the Kindwitwi Leprosy Village in Tanzania of the Universities Mission to Central Africa (now United Society for the Propagation of the Gospel), and who was to receive an Albert Schweitzer Award in 1985 for his work.

One society to which Richmal made regular donations was the Church Fellowship of Psychic Study. She was becoming interested in more mystical approaches to religion, and by no means dismissed the possibility of psychic experience. According to Miriam Place, her friend and former Bromley High School pupil, she talked of having a guardian angel who was very active in her interests, and also felt that on one or two occasions she had demonstrated second sight. (Neither Richmal nor Paul Ashbee, however, recollects her ever claiming to have second sight.) Miriam Place tells this story of one of Richmal's visits to Rottingdean. They lunched at the Dene Hotel, somewhere that they both liked very much. They were sitting at a table in the middle of the room, when apparently for no good reason, Richmal said she didn't like their table, and wanted to sit by the window. They moved, and a few seconds afterwards the overhead electric light fitting came crashing down onto the table which they had just vacated, breaking the glasses and scattering the cutlery. This could easily be explained by coincidence, but Richmal felt it was something more than that.

Richmal Ashbee comments that she heard a slightly different version of the Dene Hotel incident. She writes: 'It was the last day of Auntie's week-end stay at the hotel and she invited Miriam to lunch . . . She would normally have tipped the waiter after lunch but as Miriam was coming she did so before she arrived. Both the Head Waiter and her table waiter received generous tips and she was rather amused that they were almost fighting to please her afterwards. The Head Waiter wished to move her to one of the best tables near the window (an elderly woman on her own rarely gets a good table) while her own waiter wanted to keep her. However, the Head Waiter, of course, won, so she would have been at the window table, or been allocated it before Miriam came, and not been likely to tell her the story of the tips. Certainly the chandelier fell as described, and I am sure Auntie would have thought her Guardian Angel was working hard, but if anyone had a premonition, it was the Head Waiter, not Auntie!'

In spite of her growing interest in things psychic, she parodied them with relish in her books. The William stories are often adorned with psychic (or pseudo psychic) incidents, all of which make lively reading. One of the most amusing is William's encounter with the Society for the Encouragement of Higher Thought, in which Miss Hatherly, aunt and dragonish guardian of Robert's current inamorata, Marion, is a leading light. The society consists of three or four of those angular and over-earnest spinsters who decide to forgather in a house which, long empty, is reputed to be haunted. Of course, it happens to have been for some time the secret refuge of the Outlaws – their smugglers' den, desert island, Indian camp, battlefield and castle.

One night, with the inevitability of Greek tragedy, the Higher Thinkers gravitate towards the 'haunted' house at the same time as the Outlaws head there for a midnight feast of apples, cheesecakes, chocolate creams, currants, pickled onions and their customary brews of liquorice water and lemonade. *They* flee guiltily from Miss Hatherly's approaching footsteps; *she* falls over Robert's overnight bag (which William has brought for the purpose of carrying provisions). She reveals the bag's contents at a meeting of the society on the following day. Robert is there, coerced into attendance by Marion, and before his horrified eyes Miss Hatherly pulls out faded and (needless to say) 'very much darned' socks, other sundry garments and a truly ghastly love poem, which turns out to be not only a paean of praise for Marion, but a hymn of hate against Miss Hatherly. Marion feels she has been made a fool of, and in one of those breaking-off scenes that Richmal does so skilfully Robert's romantic aspirations are once again blighted:

'I'm going to commit suicide,' said Robert gloomily.

'I don't believe you *could*,' said Marion aggressively. 'How are you going to do it?'

'I shall drink poison.'

121

'What poison? . . .'
'Er – Prussic Acid,' said Robert.

Belief in reincarnation was something which also began to
sneak up on Richmal as she got older, but the story 'William and
the Ancient Souls' is an early skit on 'a Society dedicated to the
remembering of previous existences'. The president, who lives
in the house on one side of William's, is Miss Gregoria Mush, an
ageing spinster who has matrimonial designs on the innocuous
and mild-mannered Gregorius Lambkin, who lives on the other
side of William, and is regarded by him as an ally, because he
doesn't object to William playing in his garden. Poor little
Gregorius is forced by Gregoria into the Society of Ancient
Souls. He is – according to Gregoria – a reincarnation of Julius
Caesar; she is supposed once to have been Mary Queen of Scots.
Richmal has a wonderful time sending up the various intense
members of the society, who, garbed as Nero, Dante, Noah,
Cleopatra and Napoleon, arrive for a meeting at Gregoria's
house, spied upon by William. Gregorius Lambkin – in toga and
laurel wreath – is so limp and unhappy that his waxed
moustache begins to droop. He confides to William that though
he feels ill at ease with the Ancient Souls Miss Mush is really
being very kind to him. He asks William to say some Latin to
him, which might make him realize whether he ever really was
Julius Caesar:

'Hic, haec, hoc,' said William, obligingly.
'No', he said, 'I'm afraid it doesn't seem to mean anything
to me.'

William, with his minimal grasp of Latin, may not have been
able to provide the clue to unlock Mr Lambkin's past lives – but
he *does* manage to get him decisively off Gregoria's matrimonial
hook.

One of Richmal's precious causes – a symbol rather than an
actuality in her life – was the Golden Age that was Greece. As we
have noted, she never visited Greece, but it was in a sense one of
her secret worlds. Even in the William stories she likes to toss in

various classical allusions – 'And the plan leapt like Aphrodite, full grown, into the brains of both William and Ginger.' And Greece is very much to the fore in many of her serious novels.

In *The Wildings*, David meets Mr Canford, a rather disconcerting character, who conveys a suggestion of the fanatical. When he gets excited about Greece he barks '*God*, Boy', or just 'Boy', to David (who is a fully grown married man) in a horribly peremptory way. Canford tells David that Classical Greece holds all the true beauty of the world and that modern man has ruined everything by turning his back on the 'beauty of place and person . . . art and literature' which Classical Greece represents. David suggests that perhaps we *have* advanced since the days of Classical Greece, and Mr Canford, now very angry, points out the evils of the sewing-machine – 'good God, *sewing-machines*!' – and other modern horrors like submarines, penny-in-the-slot machines and 'that abomination they call a Picture House . . . We know a million things that the Ancient Greeks didn't, and how are we happier . . . how are we better?' David finds it all rather puzzling, but Greece is presented in a less inflated and more impressive manner in other stories by Richmal.

Two or three of Richmal's suspense stories in *Mist* use Greece as a signal of challenge or a symbol of beauty in a way that is whimsical but compelling. In the story called 'The Bronze Statuette', guests who are gathering at a country house party are shown a small bronze figure:

> It was about six inches high, and represented a young god with thick clustering curls, every muscle of his body exquisitely rendered, one leg at rest and the weight of the body thrown upon the other. In one hand were the broken remains of what had once been a bow. The small, perfect head was thrown back. The whole pose suggested power and fearlessness. It was a thing of extraordinary grace and beauty.

The statuette has a presence of its own, something highly charged, magnetized. For those who are open to its beauty, extraordinary things happen. In another story the flavour of Classical Greece comes across in human shape: Richmal was experimenting with shifts of space and time in these stories

–themes which intrigued her, and linked up with her broadening interpretation of certain aspects of her religion.

One other of Richmal's precious causes which she travestied in the William saga should be mentioned, and that is female suffrage. As noted earlier, by the time the William stories began, professional and middle-class women already had the vote; otherwise doubtless William would have been interfering with their campaigns. Richmal gives them a backward look, however, in 1936, in the story 'Pensions for Boys', which is included in *Sweet William*. Inspired by the discovery that an old age pension of ten shillings a week is available for those in the appropriate age-group, William decides that there should also be pensions for boys. He doesn't quite know how to set about achieving this, but Henry is able to make some constructive suggestions, as one of his aunts had been instrumental in getting votes for women by chaining herself to railings, making speeches from a lorry that toured the streets, and so on. The Outlaws decide to take a leaf from the suffragettes' book as far as tactics are concerned. They don't do too well with the business of putting a bomb in a church (which is one of Henry's helpful suggestions) because they have to use the only explosive which is easily available (a rather tired, old Christmas cracker), whose pathetic 'plup' is drowned by 'the Vicar's high-pitched resonant voice'. And their campaign reaches its nadir when they fall foul of the pupils of a girls' school, who resent the fact that the Outlaws' drive for pensions firmly excludes girls. William, Ginger, Henry and Douglas find themselves on the receiving end of female militancy which is reminiscent of the worst excesses of the suffragettes: 'Two hockey sticks hit William simultaneously on either side of his head. Someone thrust a ruler into Ginger's eye. The business end of a geometrical compass was jabbed into Douglas's arm.' It must be remembered, of course, that Richmal had been a suffragist rather than a suffragette, and never a militant. She obviously felt that the extremists deserved to be sent up, and set about doing this with tremendous relish.

CHAPTER 8

ON MEN AND MARRIAGE

"I think yours is the sweetest name I've ever heard,"
Robert was saying.

Richmal had been content to share her home with Gwen and her
family during the war years, but she was pleased to have it to
herself again when they moved back to their house in
Cumberland Road. She liked her own company (and of course
Ming's), was still near enough to the Dishers to see them very
frequently, and, with part-time daily help in the house and some
in the garden, could still manage the domestic routine of The
Glebe without difficulty.

By the end of the 1940s, Britain was settling down again into
peace-time, but still austere, conditions. The William books,
which had become thinner during the period of wartime paper
shortages, did not resume their pre-war look of plumpness and
well-being. Richmal, however, was happy that the books were

125

still being published regularly, and that there was a continuing demand for her adult novels.

Her brother Jack still played an important part in her life. He had been invalided out of the RAF with an ulcer in 1943, and he stayed with Richmal at The Glebe for a period after his discharge. He had not had time to write novels during the war, and decided to strike out in a new literary direction. He wrote several books of natural history, starting with *The Hunting Wasp* in 1948, and using the name of John Crompton instead of John Lambourne (his previous *nom de plume*). *The Hunting Wasp* received rave reviews from Harold Nicolson, John Betjeman, C. V. Wedgwood, Elizabeth Bowen and Brian Vesey-Fitzgerald, and his subsequent natural history books were also successful.

There seems no indication that Richmal ever met any man who made her seriously contemplate marriage or a long-term liaison. She liked men, enjoying both their company and conversation, but while she had been studying and teaching she'd operated in an all-female world which was almost a closed one. Contacts with marriageable men were few; and for girls of Richmal's generation and upbringing there would have been no question of casual encounters or 'pick-ups'. Also, Clara didn't relish being on her own, and kept her younger daughter very much under her eye, so the conventional relationship of the strong mother looking after the more delicate daughter was reinforced. Later, when Richmal might have become more independent of the attitudes of her Victorian parents, awareness of her disability might have been a barrier against making relationships with men.

Richmal's maternal (or at least auntly) instincts were fulfilled through Gwen's children. She lived a fairly quiet and home-oriented life, and didn't indulge in a great deal of socializing outside her family circle. Nevertheless, she had several much-valued friendships with women, even if she didn't see them often. These relationships were of a warm, straightforward nature, without any lesbian complications. Joan Braunholtz recalls once suggesting to Richmal that their relationship need not have been any different if one of them had been a man. Richmal replied, 'I think it would be very difficult to keep the relationship on this level.'

It is of course possible that another off-putting factor was her dislike of Gwen's husband, and the fact that her reservations about the Disher marriage turned out to be justified. Richmal seems to have put some of her resentment of Thomas into the mouth of Bridget, who in *The Innermost Room* can at times hardly contain her hatred of her sister Gloria's husband, Theo:

> Bridget was surprised at the violence of her own hatred for Theo . . . Gloria might have been so different with someone gentle and forbearing . . . Gloria was such a wonderful thing to be wasted . . . spoilt . . . And he was so spruce and sleek and pleased with himself . . . exulting in his petty victories over his typists, callous to Gloria's sufferings. If he were dead, Gloria wouldn't care. She didn't love him. She'd be her old radiant self again. It must be so easy to kill someone. Bridget could understand wanting to kill someone now. She could hardly bear to speak to him. She avoided him as much as she could. She hated him so much that she trembled from head to foot when she just met him on the stairs . . .

Richmal had always disliked Disher's heartiness and what she considered to be his hypocrisy; she felt he had cheated Gwen by womanizing from fairly early in their marriage, and that despite his professed concern for his three children he wasn't really prepared to put himself out for them and to assume the full paternal role. (Richmal Ashbee vaguely remembers her father – as a newspaper with a pair of legs sticking out underneath! She also recalls the unpleasant situation which developed in the run-up to her parents' divorce. She had to have an appendectomy, and Thomas refused to provide the money for this unless Gwen would first confirm her agreement to a divorce. Gwen had been opposed in principle to a divorce, not a surprising view for the daughter of a clergyman.)

After Thomas's defection, the households at Cumberland Road and The Glebe had a strong feminine bias. By that time Tommy Disher, the only man of the two houses, was an eighteen-year-old preparing to take up a career in the army, and his thoughts would not long be focused too fully on domestic affairs. Jack continued to take an interest in his two sisters, but he lived far away in Cornwall and wasn't able to visit either of their homes very often. Of course, for Gwen and Richmal there were still strong memories of their father, Edward, whose feelings for education and liberalism still influenced his off-spring. (The other male influence on these two households was William – who, although basically a figment of Richmal's imagination, often seemed a force to be reckoned with. And, of course, he was a money-spinner.)

Richmal might not have known a great deal about marriage at first hand, but she managed through her books to make a variety of shrewd, strange or sparkling reflections on courtship and the conjugal state. She frequently takes a conformist view, with events in her stories indicating that strong-minded women or even those who are just well poised are almost bound to come a marital cropper, while simple, vacuous and docile females are likely to inspire the lasting devotion of their menfolk:

> She had thrown herself zestfully into the furnishing of Three Elms and had made it a home of which any man should have been proud. She glanced round the room – at her treasured Sheraton and Chippendale, at the Barolozzi engravings on the white panelled walls. Her glance, passing the Queen Anne mirror above the writing-desk, showed her the reflection of her own face, pale and finely moulded with the delicate structure that spoke of race and breeding. Anger quickened her heart beats and sent a sudden trembling over her limbs. That he should be willing to leave all this for a girl whose values were probably as shoddy as her clothes ... [*The Gypsy's Baby*]

On the whole, in her adult books it is the male characters who make the rules – though there are one or two colourful bitches who know how to bend or break them.

There are frequent suggestions from the action of her novels that Richmal really did hold the view (probably a common enough one in the early 1920s) that men found intelligent women a turn-off:

Theo was amusedly contemptuous of Bridget's college career.

'Good God! What a place,' he said. 'It gives me nightmares to think of it. Sort of glorified lunatic asylum. They'll none of 'em get married and they'll regret it one day, what? Who wants a woman who's passed an exam? Enough to put any man off. However, by the look of most of 'em, they wouldn't have much chance in any case, what?' (*The Innermost Room*)

Bridget receives these crassly ugly comments in silence; there is no sign of her hitting back, as a spirited young woman in her circumstances might be expected to do. Richmal tries, however, to show the other side of the masculine coin. On one side there is Theo, coarse, arrogant and bigoted: on the other, Timothy (from *Anne Morrison*), a gentle man in holy orders (who resembles Richmal's father). Tim has married Aineen, and 'the glamour through which he saw her in that first moment never faded. He never looked with interest at any other woman. She was to him Mystery, Perfection, Romance. Even when she grew old, to him her beauty never faded.' Aineen, for her part, 'found ever fresh wonder in Timothy's love for her'. This fictional and frequently inflated man–woman relationship almost certainly derives in part from that of Richmal's parents, and seems to represent her ideal of marriage – an ideal which she found could never be realized for her.

There is a surprising sentimentality in several areas of Richmal's writings. Her natural shrewdness frequently disappeared when she wrote about sexual awareness between a man and a woman – especially when it began to ripen into 'this mysterious glory called love'.

Of course, sexual love probably was mysterious to her. It is important to remember Richmal's late Victorian upbringing, and the conditioning influences of this on her attitude to men, marriage and sex. Bridget in *The Innermost Room* is standing on the sidelines of sex, observing the intensity of her brother Derek and the look in his face when he is with Gladys, the girl he hopes to marry:

That was love. Bridget faced the thought suddenly. She had often nearly thought about it and then shirked it. It had seemed a mixture of what was too beautiful to be true and too ugly to be true. There were the stories of it that one read in books, and often they didn't ring true. And there were horrible things that one half guessed at and tried not to think about . . .

Bridget is an embodiment of the innocence (or ignorance) which late Victorian and Edwardian society expected in young middle-class girls. When, for example, she hears someone talk about a girl 'ending on the streets', she thinks this means 'selling matches and flowers and things'. She is the girl who, it may be remembered, when she was a child saw the body of a drowned man being carried along the road; this triggered off in her a multilayered, macabre fear which she can never quite cope with, and tries to repress. It is something that she calls 'the enemy'. On one occasion she is staying at the home of a college friend, and as she stands in front of the dressing-table in her nightdress, preparing for bed, the friend's father comes into her room:

> He was in pyjamas and a dressing-gown. Then he came towards her . . . Her heart gave one sickening leap and seemed to race on madly . . . She hardly recognized him . . . his mouth was smiling, a twisted sort of smile . . . Before she knew what was happening he had seized her and strained her to him, kissing her lips with long horrible sucking kisses . . . She had the impression of some savage starving animal . . . It seemed almost as if the enemy who had haunted her all her life was revealed face to face in final horror at last.

There is a lot more in this vein – hot breath, deafening heart-beats, etc. – although without the expected seduction. But the point is that Bridget's 'enemy' seems to have been revealed at last – and it is sex. From the childhood sections of the book, Bridget has always been oversensitive and a touch morbid, but there must have been many real-life Edwardian young women, of the same generation as Richmal, for whom sex came as at best an awkward and at worst a 'horrible' revelation. It seems hard to believe, however, that Richmal, so robust in many directions, could share Bridget's feelings of sex as 'the enemy'.

In writing of men and women Richmal is at her best when the approach is subtle and indirect – or exuberantly escapist, as in the William books. As an example of the former, she manages to convey in a single sentence the isolation which many women without men feel: 'She had become one of those solitary females who peck at snacks on trays because they have no men to share a decent meal with them.'

William, of course, would share a decent meal to which he was invited by any tolerantly pretty female (for he is really very susceptible). Robert, his elder brother, is even more quick to become infatuated, and in *Just – William* we meet Miss Cannon, the first embodiment on record of 'the most beautiful girl' Robert has ever met in his life. She is to come to tea with the Brown family. On her way in, she encounters William in the garden, and stays to play Red Indians with him, while Robert waits indoors on tenterhooks, longing for her arrival. During tea, William, who has also become enamoured of the lovely Miss Cannon, sits in on and interrupts Robert's awkward attempts to converse with her. Hideously embarrassed by the presence of his younger brother, Robert (and the rest of the family) try politely and surreptitiously to remove him from the scene – but, with his usual and highly articulate sense of outraged justice, William utterly humiliates Robert by declaring in a sibilant whisper that rises to a stentorian blast: 'I wasn't doin' any harm ... only *speaking* to her! ... Is no-one else ever to *speak* to her ... jus' 'cause Robert's fell in love with her?' To add insult to injury (or, rather, the other way round), William later on (again unintentionally) disrupts a picnic party, arranged by Ethel in order to cheer Robert up, at which Miss Cannon is also present. He ruins Robert's brand new bicycle in the process. No wonder the elder son of Mr and Mrs Brown is moved to make inward vows of vengeance against William, and to remark despairingly: 'You'd think four grown-up people in a house could keep a boy of William's age in order, wouldn't you? You'd think he wouldn't be allowed to go about spoiling people's lives and – and ruining their bicycles!'

Incidentally, before William even meets Miss Cannon, it becomes obvious that he has a lot to learn about the language and vocabulary of love. The following discussion between Robert and William shows their vastly varying ideas about what makes a woman 'different' or 'special':

131

'She's different from everybody else in the world,' stammered Robert ecstatically. 'You simply couldn't describe her. No-one could.'

His mother continued to darn his socks and made no comment.

Only William, his young brother, showed interest.

'*How's* she different from anyone else?' he demanded 'Is she blind or lame or sumthin?'

(This, by the way, was written before Richmal became disabled; however, her own disability was never to prevent her from using limps, sticks or crutches as aids to plots or characterizations, when appropriate.)

William's longest-lasting 'romantic interest is in Joan, the deliciously dimpled and dark-haired little girl next door. Her greatest charm in his eyes, however, is her constant appreciation of him, and her complete acceptance that he leads and she follows.

'. . . I like you better than any insect, Joan,' he said generously.

'Oh, William, do you really?' said Joan, deeply touched.

'Yes – an' I'm going to marry you when I grow up if you won't want me to talk a lot of soppy stuff that no-one can understand.'

Occasionally, however, he falls for another dark, dimpled and prepared-to-be-passive small girl. He becomes besotted by Bettine Franklin and anxious to appear to her in the part of 'the male provider':

He was one flaming mixture of embarrassment and delight. He plunged his hands into his pockets and brought out two marbles, a piece of clay, and a broken toy gun. 'You can have 'em all,' he said in reckless generosity.

(He also gives her a centipede as a token of his affection.) Richmal returns frequently to the image of the all-providing male both in the William and in her adult books. (It seems likely, however, that in her own life she was glad to have achieved a measure of fame and fortune by her own efforts, without dependence on a male protector.)

For some women, in contrast, man's only function *is* as the provider. One of Richmal's bored and cynical young things in *Felicity Stands By* declares quite seriously, 'I hate all men, but that's no reason for not marrying...'

An aspect of marriage that Richmal explores frequently in her family sagas is the plight of the bored housewife. She sees it as a common pattern that the man is busy, and the woman stuck for ways of filling in her time, especially if she has no children. Some of her female characters try to overcome boredom by shopping sprees, others by matinées, but few of them ever think of finding a job, or doing sustained voluntary work. Of course, during the 1920s when many of her novels were produced, there was a general move to try to get women back into the rigid domestic routines they had abandoned with such enthusiasm between 1914 and 1918 in order to help with the war effort. Richmal seemed to differentiate fairly strongly between the professional women in her books (whom she *did* allow to pursue careers in many instances) and the childless 'housewife', or young, unmarried middle-class girl, who was expected to stay at home until Mr Right appeared, or didn't appear, as the case might be. After the Second World War, her family sagas keep up with the social changes that it helped to instigate:

> [Her mother] had been slightly disconcerted when Jill, on leaving school, insisted on taking a secretarial training and finding a job, but she realized that since the war it had become almost a convention for a girl to have a job ... (*The Gypsy's Baby*)

And, in the same novel there is a wryly liberated lady: 'Well, I've made up my mind, I'm going to play hockey till I'm forty and then take a country cottage and keep pigs.'

There are even signs of social progress on the women's work front in the William saga. William's fascinating and fatally attractive elder sister, Ethel, managed to avoid any suggestion of working for the first thirty-five years of the books (with the exception of a short spell of voluntary work and brief service in the ATS during the Second World War). In *William and the Space Animal*, however (first published in 1956), William makes the startling statement that 'She was talkin' to mother las' night an' she said she was sick of her job [we are never told what this is] an' wanted another, so' – simply – 'I thought I'd get her another job.' Of course his plans to get her a job go awry, in much the same way as did his efforts once to get her a husband (see page 70). But it is interesting to see the type of jobs which he and the Outlaws consider for his once work-shy sister. These include working as a plain cook (but they decide she can't do that, as she's pretty), as a companion-help, as a dog-sitter, a film-star or a spy. But we know, of course, that she will in the long run stick to her true vocation – which is to flip that red-gold hair and flutter her dark-lashed violet eyes at any man who might turn out to be the exactly appropriate all-providing male.

CHAPTER 9

AFFECTIONATE AUNTIE

*"No," said William, without hesitation, "I don't like
staying with aunts."*

Richmal attended a Foyle's literary lunch in November 1954,
where she met Denise Robins, another writer of popular fiction,
who was enjoying huge success in the field of the romance novel.
Miss Robins asked her whether she had modelled the character
of William Brown on her own son, and Richmal was able to
reply, with relish: 'Hardly. You see, I'm not married.' She eased
Miss Robins's discomfiture slightly by adding, 'I am probably
the last surviving example of the Victorian professional aunt.'
That last statement can hardly be accurate, but certainly by the
beginning of the 1950s Richmal thought of herself very much as
'Auntie'. Richmal Ashbee recalls that, as 'Auntie Ray', Richmal
was something of a universal aunt; friends of the family would
find themselves addressing her as Auntie Ray, and then

adopting the more intimate form of address and calling her just 'Auntie', as her five nieces and nephews did.

There had been changes in Richmal's domestic routine since the 1940s. Her peke, Ming, had died in 1950, and been sadly mourned. Apparently she missed the wild excitement with which Ming had greeted her every time she came back to the house after being out for a few hours. She asked Joan Braunholtz, 'Where is it? Where is all Ming's love? Where has it gone?' Joan made the suggestion that there was an afterlife for animals as surely as for people, but, although Richmal accepted the idea of human survival, she didn't appear to feel that there was any immortality for dogs. At this time Joan was becoming interested in vegetarianism, which she discussed with Richmal, who replied that she too would *like* to become a vegetarian, but 'sausages are so easy'. This seemed to Joan to be a very characteristic response, as Richmal 'took things easily and naturally – didn't strain; and this, with her quick response and instant understanding made her wonderfully good company'.

Richmal was as busy as ever with her writing, and had in 1947 created a new juvenile hero called Jimmy, who was much younger than William, but cast in the same mischievous mould. Jimmy's adventures were produced specially for publication in the *Star*, an evening newspaper with a wide distribution throughout London. The stories were short, and obviously designed for younger readers than William's audience. In 1949 a number of the stories from the *Star* were collected to make a book, *Jimmy*. This was followed by another about the same character, *Jimmy Again* in 1951. (*Jimmy the Third* in 1965 comprised reprints of some of these tales.) Thomas Henry, provided the illustrations for these stories as well.

Richmal and Thomas Henry had been friends through correspondence as well as partners in the presentation of William, for many years. Strangely, however, they had not met. Both tended to avoid public engagements, but they did get together eventually, in 1954, at a luncheon arranged as one of the attractions at the Nottingham Book Festival. Their association had then already lasted for over thirty years, and it was to continue for nearly another decade, until Henry's death in 1962.

Early in the 1950s Richmal began to think about moving from The Glebe. She still loved the house and garden, but they were really too large for her to occupy on her own, especially now that she was getting older. She eventually found a house which she liked very much, Beechworth, in the picturesque village of Chislehurst, Kent, not so very far from the Dishers, whose family home was still in Cumberland Road, Bromley. Margaret continued to do very well in the fashion business and was no longer at home; Tom was employed by the Westminster Bank and still living with his mother. His younger sister, Richmal, had taken her degree at Westfield College of London University, and for several years been President of the London University Archaeological Society. She had met Paul Ashbee, a fellow archaeologist, on an excavation at St Albans, and they had married in 1952. The two Richmals were just as close after the Ashbee wedding as they had been before. 'Auntie' got on extremely well with Paul, to whom she would refer whenever she thought of writing another William story which involved an archaeological dig. Paul had been a fan of the William books for years, and as a native of Kent he was particularly intrigued to meet Richmal Crompton, and to try to find out more about the geographical settings of the places in the stories. However, William's author maintained as she had always done that although the stories might be set in Kent she had no specific villages or towns in mind when she wrote them.

Soon, in 1953, Richmal was to become a great-aunt, when the Ashbees' son Edward Gordon Crompton, was born. His sister, Catherine Richmal Crompton (Kate), came into the world in 1956, so Richmal now had a new generation of children to tell stories to, and to entertain with the lively games that she also enjoyed. (She had, too, a new small boy whose real-life antics fuelled the fictional flame of William's.) Richmal Ashbee remembers 'Auntie' playing games with Edward and Kate which involved her playing the role of hospital patient, and spending some time lying on a plank in the garden. She felt she should rescue her from these uncomfortable situations, but Richmal didn't want to be rescued. Kate Ashbee recalls great games with Auntie, in which they would re-enact Custer's Last Stand, with Richmal as Custer beseiged in the garden shed, whilst she and

Edward were the Indian attackers. She also remembers 'Auntie' writing and narrating plays for them to act, and making the children somersault over her stick in the living-room (a feat which William would surely have enjoyed performing). At this time the Ashbees were living at Chelsfield in Kent. Occasionally, if their parents were ill, or both working and away from home at the same time, Kate and Edward would go to Beechworth, and have wild games with a bottle of bubble-bath, in which 'Auntie' often had to intervene to keep the peace. They looked upon visits to Richmal Crompton as tremendous fun, particularly when she let them read William episodes as soon as she had written them. It was a very regular thing for the Ashbee family to spend time at weekends with Gwen and Richmal together. 'Auntie' also was the judge of a fancy dress competition at Edward and Kate's school.

Although Richmal did not like to take part in many public functions, she agreed to open the new Bromley Junior Library, in April 1950. A complete programme of modernization had taken place there during the previous year, and on the day of the opening the library lecture hall was full to overflowing with children, who gave her a tremendous welcome when the mayoress introduced her as the creator of 'that horrid little rascal William, so loved by us all'. Richmal urged her audience of children to experiment with reading all kinds of books, and she took the opportunity to deplore the system operated by some public libraries of grading books by age groups, as this discouraged children from finding their own reading and enjoyment levels. When Richmal had finished speaking, she led the children down the stairs from the lecture hall to the book rooms – and with so many children trailing behind her she looked rather like the Pied Piper of Hamelin.

There was a fair-sized garden at Beechworth, though not so large as the acre at The Glebe, and Richmal, with some help, continued to enjoy working in the garden. She planned her planting carefully, and worked things out well ahead in a gardening notebook. Even so, Richmal Ashbee noticed that she'd occasionally make an error in her stories by having plants grow at the wrong time. In one typescript the fictional church was decorated lavishly for the harvest festival with daffodils.

Richmal Ashbee suggested a correction, and her aunt was very happy to have her comments on this and other scripts. Auntie's system of planning for the garden tended to be just like her method of keeping her writing notes; she used the same small scraps of paper.

As well as being an active aunt to Gwen's children and grandchildren, Richmal still saw as much as she could of her brother and his family. Jack was still producing his natural history books, and writing from his home, which was now at Hawkhurst. His daughter Sarah recalls how generous an aunt and godmother Richmal Crompton was to her, particularly in 1953 when her mother went into hospital suffering from cancer and had her womb removed. At the same time Jack, who had been drinking heavily for a period, was also taken into hospital for urgent treatment. Sarah who was only 19 at the time and working in London as a secretary, received 'tremendously generous' financial help from her aunt at this difficult time.

With the knowledge that Richmal took her duties as an aunt and great-aunt so seriously, it is tempting to think that the enormous proliferation of aunts and great-aunts in the William saga came about at this time in her life. But, of course, this is not so. One has only to cast a very superficial eye over the stories to see that aunts, uncles, cousins, great-aunts, great-uncles and second cousins have always been very much in evidence. In fact, the first line of the first William story to be published in book form ('William Goes to the Pictures', from *Just – William*) begins thus:

It all began with William's aunt, who was in a good temper that morning, and gave him a shilling for posting a letter for her and carrying her parcels from the grocer's.

There are lots of aunts, too, in Richmal's adult novels. To take an example, the opening family roll-call chapters of *The Wildings* strike echoes of Galsworthy and *The Forsyte Saga*. On the whole the descriptions of aunts in the William books work better than those of them elsewhere. In the William stories Richmal Crompton conveys a great deal of characterization with remarkable economy of language. Take his Aunt Jane (or at least one variant of her; he appears to have several different aunts of this name):

> Aunt Jane was tall and prim and what she called 'house proud'. She winced at the passage of William's boots over her parquet floors even when he did not attempt to slide on them. She met all his suggestions for the employment of his time with an unfailing: 'No, William, *certainly* not.'

Aunt Jane is also the Vice-President of the New Era Society, and she has the challenging task of preparing an address for its members on 'The New Thought' while William is in the house with her. She is writing downstairs, and William is getting ready for bed upstairs, filling the air with 'horrible and raucous strains that changed with nerve-shattering suddenness from bass to tenor'. Aunt Jane has, therefore, to make instant and practical application of the New Thought to her own mind (which William's presence tears to shatters), and she says over and over again to herself, 'You are poised and in harmony. No outside disharmony can disturb you.'

But there is another Aunt Jane in William's life – *two* more Aunt Janes, in fact, and very possibly more. But these are great-aunts. In 'The Cure' (*William Again*, 1923), Mrs Brown is summoned to the supposed deathbed of Great-Aunt Jane (presumably Mrs Brown's great-aunt, and therefore William's great-great-aunt). She makes a surprising deathbed request, which is that she should see William: 'She's never seen him, you know,' Mrs Brown explains to her astounded family.

Robert voiced the general sentiment:

> 'Good Lord!' he said, 'fancy anyone wanting to see *William*!'
>   'When they're dying, too,' said Ethel in equal horror. 'One would think they'd like to die in peace, anyway.'

But after having been dragged across the sea to Ireland by his mother to Great-Aunt Jane's bedside, William virtually effects a miracle. His cousin Francis, the same age as himself, is there, white suit, golden curls and all. So are his parents, hopefully in at the death to collect some rich pickings. The two boys are left in the sick-room while Great-Aunt Jane is sleeping, and after exchanging deadly insults with each other they start to fight. Suddenly they become aware that their dying relative is sitting up in bed, eyes bright, cheeks flushed and taking a great interest in life again: 'Go it, William,' she exhorts, 'Get one in on his nose,' and so on. She recovers: William has worked a cure.

Now the strange thing is that Great-Aunt Jane turns up again in *William the Fourth* (1924) in 'Great-Aunt Jane's Treat', and we are told very firmly that 'Great-Aunt Jane was one he had never seen'. Perhaps even as she wrote these words, Richmal had a sneaking feeling that she should be checking to see if this particular relative had ever been used before. At any rate she introduces the story with this:

> William was blest with many relations, though 'blest' is not quite the word he would have used himself. They seemed to appear and disappear and reappear in spasmodic succession throughout the years. He never could keep count of them. Most of them he despised, some he actually disliked. The latter class reciprocated his feelings fervently'.

She looks in Thomas Henry's illustrations very much like the old biddy that William figuratively snatched from the jaws of death. However, this may be just because Thomas Henry thinks all great-aunts look like that. *This* Great-Aunt Jane differs from *that* Great-Aunt Jane because she has a big thing about Sin (and the other one seemed game for a good lark, or at any rate a good fight). Yet, again, William works a minor miracle: he gets her to take him to the fair for the treat she has promised him, though she fears it is sinful, and she goes wild with excitement once she gets there. She hurls coconuts with gusto, and then, in Richmal's innocent terminology, 'mounts a giant cock', which is part of a roundabout. She gets very worked up about that too, staying on it time and time again even after William has had to climb down, pale and distinctly green about the gills: 'She seemed to find the circular motion anything but monotonous. It seemed to give her a joy that all her blameless life had so far failed to produce.' She moves on to the hoop-la, the mazes, the helter-skelter (five times on that), then another go on the roundabout, another coconut shy, and turns on the switchback, the fairy boat and the wild sea. 'Crumbs!' murmurs William, 'She must have gotter inside *of iron!*' Small wonder that when Great-Aunt Jane gets back to base she can hardly believe that she has actually done all those surprising things. And small wonder too that Richmal once got a letter saying that someone's elderly relative was gravely ill, and had asked for the opportunity to read again for the last time the story about Great-Aunt Jane and Sin.

One of William's most hilarious aunt entanglements is with his mother's Aunt Emily, who comes for a week's visit, and adorns the Brown household for a month without indicating any date of departure. Claiming fragility, but actually fearfully hale and hefty, she snores violently throughout a rest upstairs every afternoon between a hearty lunch and a hearty tea. William is fascinated by her size, her appetite, and, most of all, her snore, which at its climax suggests a raging lion in pain. He quickly capitalizes on this by making it the auditory *pièce de résistance* of one of the Outlaws 'Wild Animal' shows for the local children (admission one penny). Spurred on by his audience's delighted responses, he opens up Great-Aunt Emily's bedroom and allows his public to file slowly past her immense frame – clad only in blouse and striped petticoat ('In sleep Aunt Emily was not beautiful'). He gets more and more daring and puts notices against some of the things on Aunt Emily's dressing-table: 'FAT WILD WOMAN'S TEETH, FAT WILD WOMAN'S HARE, FAT WILD WOMAN'S KOME', etc. And still she snores through it all! William is collecting pennies hand over fist and the audience keep filing in (at a penny each time) for repeat performances. At last she awakens suddenly (on the 'top note of a peal that was a pure delight to her audience'). After one horrified look around her, she springs up, shakes William till his teeth rattle, quickly dresses, then acidly asks Mr Brown (who has just awakened from *his* Sunday after-dinner nap) 'to procure a conveyance' for her. She gives Mr Brown the details about how William and co. have insulted her, Mr Brown makes muttering noises about it being *'disgraceful!'*, but, as Aunt Emily's cab departs, he presses a half-crown in William's hopeful hand.

As well as an Aunt Emily, the Browns have an Aunt Emma, who, with Uncle Frederick, comes to stay with them for

Christmas. It turns out that this is 'William's Truthful Christmas' (something hideously hazardous to be exposed to). Unusually inspired by the vicar's sermon on how untruthfulness and hypocrisy spoil the holy season, William decides to implement veracity at all times. Christmas morning goes off to a flying start when, asked by Aunt Emma if he liked her present to him (a book on Church history), William uncompromisingly replies 'No'. He goes on to explain that *his* present to her is a left-over pin-cushion from Mrs Brown's stall at the sale of work, 'an' Mother said it was no use keepin' it for nex' year because it had got so faded'. The climax of William's well-meaning but socially disastrous truthfulness comes when he encounters his Aunt Emma's aristocratic friend, Lady Atkinson, whose idea of a good Christmas gift is a large signed photograph of herself, patronizingly bestowed upon Aunt Emma and Uncle Frederick. After Lady Atkinson has smugly soaked up the general murmurs of admiration and gratitude, she turns to William.

'You . . . little boy . . . don't you think it's very like me?'

William gazed at it critically.

'It's not as fat as you are,' was his final offering at the altar of truth.

Richmal by all accounts was an ideal auntie; her reaction when she first knew that she would become an aunt may have been like that of Bridget in *The Innermost Room*: 'She'd be Aunt Bridget. She gave a little skip and hop in the road. What fun!' Richmal lets her hair down from time to time, in the William books and in her novels, about aunts who complicate Christmas and birthday present rituals by returning unwanted presents to the recipients, or doing strange things so that labels get switched and no one quite knows what they should be getting, and whether they are being consciously insulted, or not.

Felicity is another young aunt (in *Felicity Stands By*) who has a nice touch with her nephews and nieces, preferring their orange, lemon and sherbert drinks to the cocktails she has sampled on the previous evening at a night-club. One could imagine Richmal having the same chummy relationship with the Disher children. She was exactly the right sort of person to be what she described as 'a professional aunt'. She would have known exactly when to excite and stimulate her nieces and nephews, and also when to keep a low profile. She was very good at doing the latter if she thought it was correct to do so, and liked sometimes to tell the following story:

> During the war, I shared a taxi from a bus stop to Victoria Station with a mother and small boy who were strangers to me. In the course of the journey the mother mentioned that the boy was anxious to reach home in time to hear the William broadcast. My vacant expression, as I debated with myself whether or not to tell them that I wrote the stories, and reflected that they probably wouldn't believe me if I did, convinced them that I had never heard of William before, and they hastened to enlighten me. They were still describing the stories and advising me to read them when we got to Victoria. (I didn't tell them.)

On the other hand, there were times when like any other auntie – or writer, or human being – she felt the need for a little encouragement. A friend wrote to Richmal Ashbee after her aunt had died that 'the first time I met Richmal Crompton . . . I was raving about her work, and then said: "Oh, you must get sick of all this praise." She replied, "My dear, you can't lay it on too thick!" '

CHAPTER 10

ENDINGS AND BEGINNINGS

"I see someone," the crystal gazer said impressively,
"whose life is closely bound up with yours."
"Who is he?" said Ethel, with interest.

On the surface there was nothing at the end of the 1950s to suggest that the next decade would bring changes into Richmal's life. Her family were still living near her, they and she were keeping well, and, as always, there was plenty of demand for new William books. However, when her novel for adults, *The Inheritor*, was published in 1960, it marked the end of a phase; it was to be the last of her books of that nature. Apparently these novels no longer struck the right mood for contemporary readers. The words 'old-fashioned' were not uttered by Richmal's agent (Messrs A. P. Watt) but they hung in the air and their meaning sunk in. She had been very depressed when one of her adult novels had been rejected, and did not speak about this for years. She remarked realistically to friends that 'there's not

145

much call nowadays for quiet stories about families and village life – that's rather a vanished world'.

Dreaming up new escapades for William gave her plenty to do as far as writing was concerned, and although her dream child's success firmly eclipsed that of her adult books it should be remembered that for nearly forty years Richmal's family sagas and collections of short stories had commanded a considerable audience, despite the fact that fashions in popular literature are notoriously changeable.

The irony of William's ascendancy over her more serious books is neatly summed up in the story of a Dutch monk's response to her works. On leave from his monastic base, he discovered William, and lay on a sofa 'dying with laughter' at his exploits. He wrote to tell Richmal Crompton how impressed he was with the stories, and she, thinking that something less frivolous might better suit his clerical status, sent him one of her family novels. His sadly phrased response might have daunted a less determined author. 'If only these people had been good Catholics, they wouldn't have had any problems,' he replied, in acknowledgement of the book.

Read retrospectively, Richmal's family books are interesting for their conveyance of the moods and mores of the first three decades of the twentieth century. *Anne Morrison* and *The Innermost Room* in particular provide unusual insights into what life must have been like for an intelligent and questioning girl growing up in Edwardian times. The novels have sometimes been dismissed as middle-class and middle-brow, but in fact several of them deal cogently with challenging social issues. *Frost at Morning, Blue Flames* and *The Ridleys*, for example, are perceptive explorations of children from very different backgrounds, who are deprived of their proper share of parental affection. Some of the sagas span the achievements and aspirations of two or three generations, and in these, perhaps, the narrative voice is too diffuse to allow the reader to identify strongly with one character, or group. Richmal's leading characters are sometimes young girls, often mature housewives and mothers, and frequently men. On the whole the books work best when she is concentrating upon women. Whatever her family sagas might lack, they are able to put across an overall sense of optimism, warmth and well-being – which is doubtless why they are still in demand with collectors, and why some of the novels have recently been reprinted.

Richmal's last three adult novels still retain village character – casts of schoolmistresses, retired military men, ladies of the manor and 'regulars' of the local pub. There is possibly more emphasis in them on people growing older than in some of the early books. Her very last novel for adults, *The Inheritor*, is concerned with various members of the Radlett family. Nicholas, who is sixty-nine, is lame: he's had an artificial leg for twenty years, but still 'a secret resentment, bitter and ineradicable, had always prevented his coming to terms with it ... There were times when it seemed to take on a personality of its own, gloating over his disability'. Richmal must surely have been linking Nicholas's artificial leg with her own 'dead' one, and the book shows an unusual bitterness about disablement. In her earlier novels she treats the subject in a very low-key way, allowing William, for example, to make various comments about lameness, and to comment that 'all illness is boring'. She uses it both romantically and bracingly in *Felicity Stands By*, when the limp produced by Franklin's war wound 'pierces Felicity's tender heart', and he says, nonchalantly, 'I went to it [the Great War] straight from school. I just got in for the tail end of it and got off with a gammy leg.'

In *Enter – Patricia*, Richmal tackles physical problems flippantly: Patricia (though a very young woman) has recurring bouts of neuralgia, and her husband has a regular rheumatic twinge; they refer to these minor handicaps as 'Anne' and 'Herbert' respectively. And in *Kathleen and I, and, of Course, Veronica* Richmal treats the business of deformed limbs facetiously:

I was sitting at my desk trying to write a story ... I had created my hero. He was tall and handsome and – I couldn't make up my mind whether to have him clean-limbed or loose-limbed. If you've made any sort of study of the heroes of fiction you must know that they're all either the one or the other ... I can't tell you why it must be expressly stated as a virtue that his limbs are clean. One would have thought that it might be taken for granted. Nor can I tell you why it should be considered an additional attraction that his limbs should be loose. It sounds to me more like a physical deformity. But in fiction one must do as the fiction writers do. The hero must be clean-limbed or loose-limbed . . . I decided on loose-limbed. It made him seem a wobbly, jerky sort of being, but it was better than insulting him by mentioning the fact that his limbs were clean.

The three books quoted from above, of course, were all written *after* Richmal became disabled, and many other facetious or ironical references to physical handicap can be found in her stories, without any suggestion of bitterness. She was, however, seventy when *The Inheritor* was published. Almost certainly her awareness of infirmity and the ravages of old age was increasing. In 1961 she was to suffer a heart attack, and be taken to Farnborough hospital for treatment. Richmal and Paul Ashbee were away, but Gwen was able to report on their return that 'Auntie' seemed to be making a good recovery. Nevertheless, she had a long spell in hospital, and there were fears that she might be a semi-invalid for the rest of her life. On returning home Richmal appeared to recover her energy and strength, and to be as active as ever, although she remained under doctor's orders. During the 1960s she had to be admitted to hospital twice with a broken leg. This occurred once when she fell over the corner of a carpet in her own home, and once when she had an accident when visiting her brother Jack. On the second occasion it was the paralysed leg that was broken. This had been used by Richmal over the years as a kind of prop; it normally stuck out at an unusual angle, and she wrily told the story of the hospital doctors trying to set it at the customary (but for her the wrong) angle.

Richmal Ashbee realized during this period that the dead leg had been a strain on her aunt's system for a long time, causing her arteries to harden faster than they would otherwise have done. 'Auntie had put anticoagulant tablets into every garment, and the corners of her handkerchiefs, and she would take these unobtrusively.' After the heart attack and twice breaking her leg, Richmal Crompton still managed to maintain a large measure of independence. For a short time, at the family's behest, she took on a resident housekeeper, but, as soon as she felt strong enough, reverted to living alone. (She complained that she'd had to watch too many TV programmes that the housekeeper liked, but she didn't.)

Despite increasing health problems, Richmal remained fairly active in her local community. She remained a vigorous Church member throughout her life, preferring early morning communion to later services (which spared her from listening to sermons – one of her un-favourite ways of passing the time; several of her books show vicars laboriously working out their sermons, having just got as far as 'tenthly and lastly . . .'). She continued to support the Conservative Party, and amongst the letters that she kept until her death was one from Pat Hornsby Smith, the Tory MP for Chislehurst, sending congratulations to helpers who had worked for the Conservatives' 'great victory' in the recent elections. (Richmal had offered help to the local branch of the party, and they had pressed her into addressing envelopes for circulars, which was hardly an inspired use of her literary talents. Also the rather unimaginative suggestion had been made that she might like – despite the encumbrance of her 'dead' leg – to deliver leaflets. Even Richmal's campaigning zeal flagged at this point.)

In October 1962 Richmal heard of the death of Thomas Henry, at the age of eighty-three. Although they had known each other almost entirely by correspondence, there is no doubt that his death represented to her the loss of an extremely good and dear friend. For forty years they had collaborated on the presentation of William, who had, in a sense, been their joint baby, even though he was primarily the product of Richmal's imagination. Thomas Henry had died suddenly, while working on a William drawing. As well as illustrating the William story for over four decades he had contributed regularly to numerous periodicals including *London Opinion*, the *Tatler* and *Punch* (which once published forty-five of his cartoons in a year). Thomas Henry was born in the Nottingham mining village of Eastwood, in a house opposite the one in which six years later D. H. Lawrence was to be born. His family moved to Nottingham when Thomas was a baby, and he lived in or near there throughout his life. He contributed to the *Nottingham Guardian* for over fifty years and had his paintings exhibited in several galleries. He drew most of the *Happy Mag.* covers, designed book jackets and had a hand in the creation of the sailor trademark of Player's Navy Cut cigarettes.

Thomas Henry had a daughter by his first wife, who predeceased him and he then married again. He had no other children. According to his daughter, Marjorie Fisher, he was 'very fond of small boys and their mischievous ways, and was quite a William himself when young ... he liked to play pranks ... He enjoyed illustrating the William books most of all but he also liked painting landscapes in watercolours.' Thomas Henry's staunch loyalty to the eleven-year-old desperado had been illustrated some years earlier in connection with the *Woman's Own* picture-strip series that had been featuring William since the end of the 1940s. This was drawn by Thomas Henry, and Richmal had such faith in his judgement about William's presentation that, once the strip was launched, she left it to him to think up ideas for the strip, as well as to draw the pictures. He carried out his brief extremely conscientiously, but occasionally his inspiration dried up, and he had to accept ideas from the magazine's editorial staff. These were not always to his liking. For a period during the 1950s he felt that the storylines were becoming 'un-William-like', and he wrote to Richmal, informing her that he had been having 'a tussle' with the editorial people, in order to preserve William's reputation, and 'to save him being sent to an approved school.' After all, he went on to say, William 'was neither a thief nor an irresponsible half-wit'. Richmal weighed in heavily on Thomas Henry's side, and William's authentic personality was quickly and amicably re-established in the strip.

After Thomas Henry's death the illustrations in the books (and the William picture-strip) were taken over by Henry Ford, who made valiant attempts to imitate those of his predecessor, without ever managing entirely to emulate their elegance and style. *William and the Witch*, published in 1964, contained the last of Thomas Henry's pictures, and several by Henry Ford. Through her agents Richmal asked to see Ford's illustrations in advance of publication; she was sent the galley proofs, on which she made the following comments:

I think that, on the whole, the artist has captured the spirit of the stories and characters very well indeed. Only two of them, in my opinion, need slight alteration. In the illustration of the Hoop-la stall – galley 32 – William's head looks too big for his body (actually the length of the head is almost the same as the length of his shin from knee to heel) and in galley 33 (frontis-piece) William's features seem a little askew. His eye is too large and too round (he is supposed to be looking down) and his mouth is right on one side of his face. I think that these two sketches could be altered without much difficulty. Perhaps you will ask your artist to give these points his consideration.

As can be seen from the finished copies of *William and the Witch*, Richmal's suggestions were faithfully carried out.

At an age when death was claiming several of her con-temporaries, she especially appreciated the company of younger members of her family like her great-nephew, Edward Ashbee, and his sister Kate. Kate Ashbee recalls that at family get-togethers 'Grannie' (Gwen) liked to 'look after' the adults, leaving 'Auntie' (Richmal) free to give time to the children. To Kate and Edward she seemed always a kindred spirit. Richmal often expresses in her books the conspiratorial bond between youth and age. In 'The Circus', a story from *William Again*, unknown to anyone else in the household William illicitly visits the circus one night, taking with him his old and apparently fearfully frail Grandfather Moore, who is visiting the Browns. The young boy and the old man, both of whom are supposed to be in bed, are transported in equal measure by the delights of the circus, which include the ring-master's twirling moustachios, the antics of the red-nosed clowns and, of course, the exploits of the animals. Most of all they are thrilled by the golden hair, red cheeks, white tights and short, frilly skirts of the bareback rider. William quickly decides *not* to marry the little girl next door after all, but to become a clown and make the bareback rider his wife:

'Golly,' he breathed.
'Isn't she fine?' said Grandfather Moore.
'Isn't she *just*?' said William.

They walk home 'almost dazed and drunk with happiness', knowing that retribution will probably be visited on them both in the morning, but not caring. However, at breakfast the next day it is obvious that no one has discovered their secret outing. Aunt Lillian (whose only preoccupation is Grandfather Moore's health) says smugly, '*Doesn't* he look well this morning? . . . A good long night does him no end of good. I'm so glad I persuaded him to go to bed directly after tea . . .' And we are told, simply, that 'William's eyes and Grandfather Moore's eyes met for a second across the table.'

Boys and boyhood continued to intrigue Richmal. She kept a collection of quotations on this subject, and from 1959 retained a cutting from the *New York Times*, about a book called *And to Be a Boy Eternal*. This comprised an assemblage of comments on boyhood, inspired by letters of Mark Twain which had recently come to light. Richmal must have relished the answer to a twelve-year-old boy's question on whether Mark Twain would like to re-live his own boyhood. Mark Twain had replied that the answer was in the negative unless the following 'modifying stipulations' were met: that it should always be summer with magnolias in bloom; that he be a cub pilot on a Mississippi riverboat, and that he'd not be given the 'forlorn' midnight watch. Richmal had written (typically, on the back of an envelope) Plato's description, 'A boy is, of all wild beasts, the most difficult to tame', and Charles Lamb's 'Boys are capital fellows in their own way, but unwholesome companions for grown people', followed by Alan Beck's 'A boy is a composite – he has the appetite of a horse, the digestion of a sword-swallower, the curiosity of a cat, the lungs of a dictator . . . the shyness of a violet, the enthusiasm of a firecracker and, when he makes anything, he has five thumbs on each hand.'

What is perhaps a surprising description of one particular boy was suggested to Richmal by Joan Braunholtz in a letter dated 18 November 1968 (she had heard Richmal's broadcast about William on that day):

What you said about William made me think that he is a sort of 'Prodigal Son', I mean, he is the primitive, natural, spontaneous, adventurous part of ourselves which we all have to repress in order to fit into conventional society. But he is capable of re-birth, like the Prodigal Son.

Rebirth, both actual and symbolic, had become a strong preoccupation with Richmal during the 1960s. She had touched on the subject of reincarnation in some of her earlier books, in 'William and the Ancient Souls' from *More William* (1922), in several stories from *Mist* (1928) and in *The Innermost Room* (1923). In the last-named book, Bridget – as she so often does – dwells on the negative aspects of life:

> Sometimes when she was overtired she woke in the night with the old horror of Eternity – of going on and on and on and on – so terribly worse than death ... She would lie awake, turning restlessly from side to side, and it was as if all the suffering of all the ages lay heavy upon her. Her thoughts went right back down the centuries ... always cruelty and suffering ... the early Christian martyrs ... the rack slowly pressing the joints ... the knife entering the flesh ... in fevered imagination, panting with the imagined pain, she recanted ... tried again ... recanted ... Then other things, things of the Middle Ages ... people left in airless dungeons for years with rats and filth ... people put to death in terrible ways ... and it was just chance it was not she ... just chance she had been born in an age of mercy ...
>
> She tossed from side to side ... it wasn't only in ancient times ... things happened now every day ... terrible things ... a woman robbed and killed horribly in a field only last week ... all the beauty and joy gone from life ..., it might have been anyone ... it might have been herself. Suppose that at some time everyone had to undergo it, the supreme horror of pain and terror. Suppose there was something in Reincarnation and in one life or another it came to everyone ...

A little later in the same book there is a rather more hopeful reference to the concept of rebirth:

> 'Life's jolly unfair all round ...'
> They sat silent – overwhelmed with a crushing sense of the

relentlessness of fate, suddenly frightened by the unseen forces of destiny.

'I wonder what happens to those people,' said Bridget, slowly. 'The people who've never had a chance?'

Susan moved her dark graceful head . . .

'That's why I like the idea of Reincarnation,' she said. 'Perhaps they get a chance next time.'

In these early books, belief in reincarnation is posited, but pushed aside as something rather fearful (in the serious novels) or terribly funny (in the William stories). Prophetically, in *Mist*, someone remarks: 'It's strange how when you're old, the things that have happened to you sort themselves out into real and not real, and seem quite different from what they seemed at the time.' In later life, when Richmal questioned more and more deeply the nature of truth, reality and illusion, she appears to have accepted a belief in reincarnation.

During the early 1960s she became interested in a 'Meditation Group for the New Age' (a serious movement, whose name nevertheless sounds a little bit like one of the hilarious Higher Thought groups that she so often sent up in the William tales). The group, a non-sectarian organization, stressed creative thinking, right relationships and universalism. Richmal obtained its literature from the Tunbridge Wells head-quarters, and also became a regular attender at an informal local meditation and discussion group (which seems to have been linked with the Church's Fellowship for Psychical Studies). She grew seriously interested in mysticism (at first in a Christian, and then in a broader, framework) and the occult. 'One needs an occasional rest from occult reading – the impact is so terrific,' she wrote to Joan Braunholtz, who shared this interest, in 1962. She studied the works of Western mystics like Thomas Traherne, Thomas Merton and Mother Julian of Norwich, and she acquired a comprehensive collection of mystical books which she read and discussed by letter with Joan. (This collection includes, amongst many others, the *Bhagavad Gita*, some mantric poetry, and books by Kierkegaard, Simone Weil, Teilhard de Chardin, Rudolf Steiner, Max Freedom and the Revd Leslie Weatherhead.) With these books Richmal kept two separate definitions of mysticism – that of the *Oxford Dictionary*, 'the spiritual apprehension of truths beyond the understanding', and of Evelyn Underhill, 'the approach to the Source of Being through a heightened awareness'. She had written (on the back of an invitation card from the directors of Harvey Nichols & Co. to a showing of the Marchesa Olga de Gresy's jersey suits, resort and evening wear) some prayers and meditations, including St Patrick's 'Breastplate': 'Christ within me, Christ behind me, Christ before me', etc. Correspondence with friends (kept with these books and notes) indicated that she was also extremely interested in dreams.

Two women with a vigorous interest in reincarnation who influenced Richmal were Helen Greaves, an author, and Frances Banks, a teacher-nun. The latter, who had been at college with Richmal and introduced her to various aspects of occultism and yoga, died in 1965; she was then supposed to have psychically conveyed the text of a book about her afterlife, called *Testimony of Light*, to her friend Helen Greaves, who wrote it down and had it published. (This too sounds like something from an 'Ancient Souls' or 'Higher Thought' episode from a William book – but at this stage in her life Richmal was taking it very seriously.)

She was sometimes assailed by doubts. Paul Ashbee comments that for a time she became morbidly fascinated by the work of Hieronymous Bosch, and later by the bloody, writhing and tortured Christs of other early painters. 'Brought up on cosy, C. of E. late-19th-Century art – tranquil pictures and Burne-Jones stained glass', she was haunted by those tortured representations of Christ, which she linked with the horrors of the Nazi concentration camps.

Torture and cruelty had also preyed on Richmal's mind when as a young woman she wrote about Bridget's preoccupation with brutality in *The Innermost Room*. This morbid aspect of her nature (to which she rarely succumbed) was in marked contrast to the more frequently manifest relaxed geniality. Paul and Richmal Ashbee recall 'Auntie' as a wonderful conversationalist, who unobtrusively encouraged others to speak, even if they were shy. 'We'd be laughing constantly at her remarks; she could somehow "up" and "down" the level of these so that Kate and Edward [their children] were included as fully as the adults.' She made witty play on words and situations, from trivial to public events, but she was never malicious 'or even sharp. She never felt superior to anyone, even if she was sending them up.'

Gwen, as well as her sister, looked into other doctrines than the conventionally Christian. But both she and Richmal remained practising members of the Anglican Church until the end of their lives. Like John Wesley, each of them could say that she 'lived and died a member of the Church of England'. Richmal wrote to Joan Braunholtz in 1966 that she hoped one day to tackle the abridged but 'most formidable' *Decline and Fall of the Roman Empire*. 'I thought, when I got it, I'd keep it for my last illness, but lately I've been thinking that I'd like a less lengthy last illness, and might as well take the plunge now!'

Perhaps Richmal *did* have a touch of second sight! She never did have a lengthy last illness, and she did seem to know just when she was going to die – although, when driving on a foggy day a week or two before her death, she thought prematurely at one moment: 'Enid Blyton, here I come!' (Enid Blyton, who was almost a contemporary of Richmal's, had died at the end of November 1968.) Richmal's 1969 engagement diary projected several activities for the first few days of the year, but absolutely *nothing* beyond 11 January – the day on which she was to die. Audrey Carr's name was written in for that date, but only blank pages followed. There was something uncanny about this, particularly because in previous years it was obvious that she had certain very regular commitments (like the meditation group) which she would pencil in weeks in advance.

She had spent Christmas Day with the family at Gwen's and joined in the celebration of Edward's birthday on 27 December. She wrote to Joan Braunholtz on 29 December that she 'was interested to read in the *Daily Telegraph* that Russian and American scientists deduced from certain mysterious signs that there might be a *higher civilization* than our own at other points in the universe. One has always hoped that there might be, hasn't one? . . . the moon business is rather thrilling, not in itself, but because it might be a jumping off ground for something bigger.'

The Ashbees had been house-hunting for some time in the Norwich area because Paul was to take up in the following May an appointment as archaeologist and secretary of the Centre of East Anglian Studies, at the University of East Anglia. In the afternoon of 10 January Richmal Crompton went over to their home at Chelsfield, as she had so often done. They dined (on rump steak and chocolate eclairs, one of her favourite meals) and she insisted on washing up afterwards. Kate, going into the kitchen, found her great-aunt getting up off the floor. Richmal said that she had just slipped, however, and begged her not to worry the others by mentioning it.

Richmal Ashbee had noticed during the course of the evening that her aunt looked tired. Paul recalls that Richmal Crompton was a great one for ceremonial leave-takings, 'rather in the Jane Austen tradition of putting the departing guests into carriages'. Their farewells to 'Auntie' were always of this nature. But on this last occasion it was well after nine o'clock when she was leaving, Kate and Edward were already in bed, and Paul had a telephone call from the other end of the country just as she was proposing to go. He suggested ringing off – but she urged him to take the call. Richmal Ashbee saw her aunt to her car. Now, many years afterwards, Paul still regrets that he was robbed of the opportunity to say his usual 'Goodbye; take care now!' to 'Auntie'.

She drove herself home, and, feeling very tired on her arrival, didn't even unload the car or shut the garage door. The next morning Richmal telephoned Mr and Mrs John Rhodes, two very local friends, who came over to help her. She told them she'd been ill (in fact, she'd had a heart attack in bed), but she was up and fully dressed. The Rhodes called her doctor, and Richmal was admitted to Farnborough hospital at about 12.30. She hadn't wanted to worry Gwen or the Ashbees, who were told by telephone that she was in hospital but that all was well. Richmal Ashbee had an estate agent calling to see their house, in connection with the forthcoming move, and he was late. It was 3.20 p.m. before she could telephone the hospital. By then 'Auntie' was dead.

The Ashbees were not only grieved but stunned. And Richmal's death was a considerable shock to Gwen. (She and Richmal had been saying to each other only a day or two beforehand how much they'd 'like to see mother again'.)

Richmal's funeral service took place at St Nicholas's Church,

Chislehurst, on 16 January 1969, on 'an overcast but not an umbrella day'. The service was conducted by the Revd G. S. Budgett, a personal friend of Richmal's. The cremation followed at Eltham, where the Rector of Chislehurst, the Revd S. H. Adams, conducted a short service. Family mourners included Gwen, Tommy and Margaret Disher, Paul, Richmal and Edward Ashbee, and Jack's children, David and Sarah, with her husband Tom Welbourn, and Richmal's older cousin Sir John Wrigley, and his son Martin. Also present were Mrs Paul (later Lady Sybil) Osmond, representing St Elphin's; Miss M. E. Hardwick, representing the Girls' Public Day School Trust and Bromley High School; Miss Audrey Carr, representing Friends of the Girls' Public Day School Trust; and representatives of many of the religious and charitable organizations that Richmal had supported. Also several of her friends and acquaintances, including Mrs Watts, her domestic help for some twenty years.

Jack had been too ill to be present at the ceremony. Amongst the letters left by Richmal was one from her brother dated 27 December 1968. He addressed her as 'Dear old R.', and explained that he'd had 'another blackout' and fallen on the back of his head. He'd lain on the floor till daylight 'all messed up and bloody', and then been able to telephone the doctor. He'd gone to Tunbridge Wells hospital, where they had found no breaks but severe bruising. He was writing from his daughter Sarah's home at Crowborough: 'Sarah has been marvellous', etc.

Jack died of a stroke, not long after Richmal. Gwen lived to be over ninety. Her son Tom Disher, who never married, lived with, and looked after, her at the Cumberland Road house until she died of a heart attack in 1981. Surprisingly, Tom, who was extremely robust and athletic, died suddenly in 1983.

Richmal Crompton left nearly £60,000, a considerable sum for the time. Her niece received some seventy letters of condolence, and the tributes to her aunt were moving and wholehearted. Some of the writers were personal friends of Richmal Crompton's; others were enthusiastic readers of her books, who felt that in her death they'd lost someone they loved.

She left a batch of recent unanswered letters, several files and boxes of notes and clippings and manuscripts. Amongst the press cuttings which she'd kept was one from the *Bolton Evening*

News dated 10 April 1963 about a reader's letter. This referred to the recently reported ban on the William books by a St Pancras librarian, and pointed out that 'Miss Cooke, the Lancashire County Librarian, also banned the William stories' (reasons were not given). To counterbalance this gloomy little cutting, perhaps, Richmal had retained a much more cheerful one from the *Daily Mail* of 5 October 1968. This featured a photograph of the young Viscount Linley, 'looking rather like that lovable scamp, "Just William" '.

Richmal was still writing about 'that lovable scamp' (or, as she sometimes called him, 'that little savage') till the day before she died. Richmal Ashbee found jottings 'on odd bits of paper' all over the house, which she finally realized were different versions of passages for the story she was engaged in writing. This was 'William's Foggy Morning', one of the tales that eventually appeared (finished off by Richmal Ashbee from her aunt's notes) in the last of all the William books, *William the Lawless*, in 1970.

Some fifty years on from the first William stories, this thirty-eighth book of the series features precious causes, including the Extra Dimensions and Perfect Harmony Community, and a Brighter Thought Movement. But, in an age of wider tolerance, these are less amusing than the gawky Greek dancers, flamboyant aesthetes and intense apostles of elevating ideas that Richmal created in the 1920s. William continues to wreak havoc on stuffy spinsters, nervous clerics, and dyspeptic ex-military men, but these village archetypes seem less peppery than in their heyday. Aunts still get a mention here and there, with William (having so many of them) understandably vague about some of their names.

The stories remain immensely readable. Time in William's unnamed village has *almost* stood still – and the golden glow that hung over it through the twenties, thirties and forties has lost none of its lustre. It is cheering to reflect that *William the Lawless*, written at the very end of Richmal's life, still treats the past with affection, the present with relish, and the future with optimism: 'I thought' (says William in 'a tone of satisfaction') 'we'd done pretty well everythin' that could be done, but somethin' gen'rally comes along that we've not done before.'

159

For Richmal Crompton, just as for her most famous creation William Brown, every ending was a new beginning, every challenge a fresh hope. Some part of her resilient spirit is sealed for ever into the saga that started as a pot-boiler, and has become a classic.

APPENDIX

PUBLISHED WORKS OF RICHMAL CROMPTON

Publications for Children

Novels and Short Stories

The first twenty William books are currently available in both hardback and paperback from Macmillan.

All the William books until 1964 were illustrated by Thomas Henry.

Just William. London, Newnes, 1922.
More William. London, Newnes, 1922.
William Again. London, Newnes, 1923.
William the Fourth. London, Newnes, 1924.
Still William. London, Newnes, 1925.
William the Conqueror. London, Newnes, 1926.
William the Outlaw. London, Newnes, 1927.
William in Trouble. London, Newnes, 1927.
William the Good. London, Newnes, 1928.
William. London, Newnes, 1929.
William the Bad. London, Newnes, 1930.
William's Happy Days. London, Newnes, 1930.
William's Crowded Hours. London, Newnes, 1931.
William the Pirate. London, Newnes, 1932.
William the Rebel. London, Newnes, 1933.
William the Gangster. London, Newnes, 1934.
William the Detective. London, Newnes, 1935.
Sweet William. London, Newnes, 1936.
William the Showman. London, Newnes, 1937
William the Dictator. London, Newnes, 1938.
William and A.R.P. (Newnes, 1939); as *William's Bad Resolutions* (1956).
Just William: The Story of the Film. London, Newnes, 1939.
William and the Evacuees. London, Newnes, 1940; as *William the Film Star* (1956).
William Does His Bit. London, Newnes, 1941.

William Carries On. London, Newnes, 1942.

William and the Brains Trust (Newnes, 1945).

Just William's Luck. London, Newnes, 1948.

Jimmy, illustrated by Lunt Roberts. London, Newnes, 1949.

William the Bold. London, Newnes, 1950.

Jimmy Again, illustrated by Lunt Roberts. London, Newnes, 1951.

William and the Tramp. London, Newnes, 1952.

William and the Moon Rocket. London, Newnes, 1954.

William and the Space Animal. London, Newnes, 1956.

William's Television Show. London, Newnes, 1958.

William the Explorer. London, Newnes, 1960.

William's Treasure Trove. London, Newnes, 1962.

William and the Witch, illustrated by Thomas Henry and Henry Ford. London, Newnes, 1964.

Jimmy the Third, illustrated by Lunt Roberts. London, Armada, 1965.

William and the Pop Singers, illustrated by Henry Ford. London, Newnes, 1965.

William and the Masked Ranger, illustrated by Henry Ford. London, Newnes, 1966.

William the Superman, illustrated by Henry Ford. London, Newnes, 1968.

William the Lawless, illustrated by Henry Ford. London, Newnes, 1970.

Play

William and the Artist's Model. London, J. Garnet Miller, 1956.

Several other William titles appeared in 1965 which were compilations of stories from earlier William books.

Publications for Adults

Novels

The Innermost Room. London, Melrose, 1923.

The Hidden Light. London, Hodder and Stoughton, 1924.

Anne Morrison. London, Jarrolds, 1925.

The Wildings. London, Hodder and Stoughton, 1925.

David Wilding. London, Hodder and Stoughton, 1926.

The House. London, Hodder and Stoughton, 1926; as *Dread Dwelling*, New York, Boni and Liveright, 1926.

Millicent Dorrington. London, Hodder and Stoughton, 1927.

Leadon Hill. London, Hodder and Stoughton, 1927.

Enter – Patricia. London, Newnes, 1927.

The Thorn Bush. London, Hodder and Stoughton, 1928.
Roofs Off! London, Hodder and Stoughton, 1928.
The Four Graces. London, Hodder and Stoughton, 1929.
Abbot's End. London, Hodder and Stoughton, 1929.
Blue Flames. London, Hodder and Stoughton, 1930.
Naomi Godstone. London, Hodder and Stoughton, 1930.
Portrait of a Family. London, Macmillan, 1932.
The Odyssey of Euphemia Tracy. London, Macmillan, 1932.
Marriage of Hermione. London, Macmillan, 1932.
The Holiday. London, Macmillan, 1933.
Chedsy Place. London, Macmillan, 1934.
The Old Man's Birthday. London, Macmillan, 1934; Boston, Little Brown, 1935.
Quartet. London, Macmillan, 1935.
Caroline. London, Macmillan, 1936.
There Are Four Seasons. London, Macmillan, 1937.
Journeying Wave. London, Macmillan, 1938.
Merlin Bay. London, Macmillan, 1939.
Steffan Green. London, Macmillan, 1940.
Narcissa. London, Macmillan, 1941.
Mrs. Frensham Describes a Circle. London, Macmillan, 1942.
Weatherley Parade. London, Macmillan, 1944.
Westover. London, Hutchinson, 1946.
The Ridleys. London, Hutchinson, 1947.
Family Roundabout. London, Hutchinson, 1948.
Frost at Morning. London, Hutchinson, 1950.
Linden Rise. London, Hutchinson, 1952.
The Gypsy's Baby. London, Hutchinson, 1954.
Four in Exile. London, Hutchinson, 1955.
Matty and Dearingroydes. London, Hutchinson, 1956.
Blind Man's Buff. London, Hutchinson, 1957.
Wiseman's Folly. London, Hutchinson, 1959.
The Inheritor. London, Hutchinson, 1960.

Short Stories

Kathleen and I, and, of Course, Veronica. London, Hodder and Stoughton, 1926.
A Monstrous Regiment. London, Hutchinson, 1927.
Mist and Other Stories. London, Hutchinson, 1928.
The Middle Things. London, Hutchinson, 1928.

Felicity Stands By. London, Newnes, 1928.
Sugar and Spice and Other Stories. London, Ward Lock, 1929.
Ladies First. London, Hutchinson, 1929.
The Silver Birch and Other Stories. London, Hutchinson, 1931.
The First Morning. London, Hutchinson, 1936.

INDEX